AAT
TUTORIAL TEXT

Intermediate Unit 6

Cost Information

August 1997 edition

The fifth edition of this Tutorial Text has the following improvements.

- Full account has been taken of recent Central Assessments

- The text contains expanded guidance on cost coding, labour turnover and variances

- Coverage of other topics has been updated or revised

BPP Publishing
August 1997

First edition 1993
Fifth edition August 1997

ISBN 0 7517 6085 4(Previous edition 0 7517 6064 1)

British Library Cataloguing-in-Publication Data
A catalogue record for this book
is available from the British Library

Published by

BPP Publishing Limited
Aldine House, Aldine Place
London W12 8AW

We are grateful to the Lead Body for Accounting for permission to reproduce extracts from the Standards of Competence for Accounting.

Printed by Ashford Colour Press, Gosport, Hants

Page

INTRODUCTION (v)

How to use this Tutorial Text - Standards of competence - Assessment structure -
BPP meets the AAT

PART A: MATERIALS, LABOUR AND EXPENSES

1   Cost information   3

2   Materials   11

3   Labour costs   35

4   Expenses   51

5   Absorption costing   65

PART B: BOOKKEEPING ENTRIES FOR COST INFORMATION

6   Bookkeeping entries for cost information   91

PART C: COSTING METHODS

7   Job, batch and process costing   107

PART D: STANDARD COSTING AND VARIANCE ANALYSIS

8   Standard costing   123

9   Variance analysis   133

INDEX   157

ORDER FORM

REVIEW FORM & FREE PRIZE DRAW

HOW TO USE THIS TUTORIAL TEXT

This Tutorial Text has been designed to help students and lecturers get to grips as effectively as possible with the standards of competence for Unit 6 *Recording cost information*. Coverage of the units and elements of competence in the Text is indicated on pages (vi) to (x) by chapter references set against each performance criteria.

This Tutorial Text is designed to be used alongside BPP's Unit 6 *Cost Information* Workbook which provides exercises on the material covered in the Text, together with Devolved Assessments and Central Assessments.

Practice Exercises

As you complete each chapter of this Tutorial Text, work through the *Practice Exercises* in the corresponding section of the *Cost Information* Workbook. Once you have completed all of the Sessions of Practice Exercises, you will be in a position to attempt the Devolved Assessments.

Devolved Assessments

The tasks involved in a *Devolved Assessment* will vary in length and complexity, and there may be more than one 'scenario'. If you complete all of the Devolved Assessments in the Workbook, you will have gained practice in all parts of the elements of competence included in Unit 6. You can then test your competence by attempting the Trial Run Devolved Assessment, which is modelled on the type of assessment actually set by the AAT.

Central Assessments

Of course you will also want to practise the kinds of task which are set in the *Central Assessments*. The main Central Assessment section of the BPP Workbook includes all the AAT Central Assessments set from December 1993 to December 1994, and by doing them you will get a good idea of what you will face in the assessment hall. When you feel you have mastered all relevant skills, you can attempt the five Trial Run Central Assessments in the Workbook. These consist of the June 1995 – June 1997 Central Assessments. Provided you are competent, they should contain no unpleasant surprises, and you should feel confident of performing well in your actual Central Assessment.

A note on pronouns

On occasions in this Tutorial Text, 'he' is used for 'he or she', 'him' for 'him or her' and so on. Whilst we try to avoid this practice, it is sometimes necessary for reasons of style. No prejudice or stereotyping according to gender is intended or assumed.

STANDARDS OF COMPETENCE

The competence-based Education and Training Scheme of the Association of Accounting Technicians (AAT) is based on an analysis of the work of accounting staff in a wide range of industries and types of organisation. The Standards of Competence for Accounting which students are expected to meet are based on this analysis.

The Standards identify the *key purpose* of the accounting occupation, which is to operate, maintain and improve systems to record, plan, monitor and report on the financial activities of an organisation, and a number of *key roles* of the occupation. Each key role is subdivided into *units of competence*. By successfully completing assessments in specified units of competence, students can gain qualifications at NVQ/SVQ levels 2, 3 and 4, which correspond to the AAT Foundation, Intermediate and Technician stages of competence respectively.

Intermediate stage key roles and units of competence

The key roles and unit titles for the AAT Intermediate stage (NVQ/SVQ level 3) are set out below.

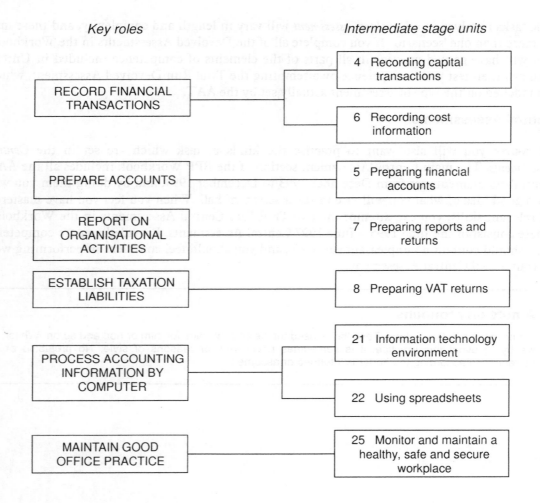

Key roles	Intermediate stage units
RECORD FINANCIAL TRANSACTIONS	4 Recording capital transactions
	6 Recording cost information
PREPARE ACCOUNTS	5 Preparing financial accounts
REPORT ON ORGANISATIONAL ACTIVITIES	7 Preparing reports and returns
ESTABLISH TAXATION LIABILITIES	8 Preparing VAT returns
PROCESS ACCOUNTING INFORMATION BY COMPUTER	21 Information technology environment
	22 Using spreadsheets
MAINTAIN GOOD OFFICE PRACTICE	25 Monitor and maintain a healthy, safe and secure workplace

Units and elements of competence

Units of competence are divided into *elements of competence* describing activities which the individual should be able to perform.

Each element includes a set of *performance criteria* which define what constitutes competent performance. Each element also includes a *range statement* which defines the situations, contexts, methods etc in which the competence should be displayed.

Supplementing the standards of competence are statements of *knowledge and understanding* which underpin competent performance of the standards.

The elements of competence for Unit 6: *Recording cost information* are set out below. The performance criteria and range statements for each element are listed first, followed by the knowledge and understanding required for the unit as a whole. Performance criteria and areas of knowledge and understanding are cross-referenced below to chapters in the *Cost Information Tutorial Text*.

Unit 6: Recording cost information

6.1 Operate and maintain a system of accounting for material costs

Performance criteria	*Chapter(s) in this Text*
1 Data are correctly coded, analysed and recorded	2, 6
2 Standard costs for materials are established in accordance with the organisation's procedures	8
3 Materials issued from stores are correctly priced in accordance with the organisation's policy	2
4 Materials issued are systematically checked against the organisation's overall usage and stock control practices and unusual issues reported to management	2
5 Timely information on materials usage is accurately presented to management	2, 9
6 Any queries are either resolved immediately or referred to the appropriate person	2, 9

Range statement

1   Materials issued from stores within the organisation

2   Standard and actual material costs

3   Direct and indirect materials costs

6.2 Operate and maintain a system of accounting for labour costs

Performance criteria	*Chapter(s) in this Text*
1 Data are correctly coded, analysed and recorded	3, 6
2 Standard labour costs are established in accordance with the organisation's procedures	8
3 Labour costs are calculated in accordance with the organisation's policies and procedures	3
4 Timely information relating to labour utilisation is presented accurately to management	3, 9
5 Staff working in operational departments are consulted to resolve any queries in the data	3, 9

Range statement

1   Employees of the organisation on the payroll. Self employed persons excluded
2   Labour costs: salaried labour, payment by results, time rates
3   Standard and actual labour costs
4   Direct and indirect labour costs

6.3 Operate and maintain a system of accounting for expenses

Performance criteria	*Chapter(s) in this Text*
1 Data are correctly coded, analysed and recorded	4, 6
2 Standard costs for expenses are established in accordance with the organisation's procedures	8
3 Information relating to expenses is accurately and clearly presented to management	4, 9
4 Staff working in operational departments are consulted to resolve any queries in the data	4, 9

Range statement

1   Expenses: revenue and capital expenditure invoiced to the organisation, depreciation charges

2   Actual and standard costs for expenses

     [Note that this element is concerned with the initial recording of the expenses. Reallocation (as part of overhead apportionment/absorption) is covered in 6.4)]

6.4 Operate and maintain a system for the apportionment and absorption of indirect costs (overheads)

Performance criteria	Chapter(s) in this Text
1 Overhead costs are correctly attributed to direct cost centres and cost units in accordance with agreed methods or apportionment and absorption	5
2 Adjustments for under/over recorded overheads are made in accordance with established procedures	5, 6, 9
3 Methods of overhead apportionment and absorption are reviewed at regular intervals in discussion with senior staff	5
4 Staff working in operational departments are consulted to resolve any queries in the data	5

Range statement

1   Indirect costs (overheads) which need to be attributed to cost centres/cost units - indirect materials, indirect labour and indirect expenses.

2   Methods of apportionment: floor area, number of employees, time taken, use of service.

Unit 6: Knowledge and understanding

The column headed Elements indicates the elements of Unit 6 under which the area of knowledge and understanding is listed in the Standards of Competence.

The business environment	Elements	Chapter(s) in this Text
● Main types of materials: (see Range Statement)	6.1	2
● Methods of payment for employees	6.2	3
● Main types of expenses: expenses directly charged to cost units (eg sub-contracting charges), indirect expense, depreciation charges	6.3	4

Accounting techniques		
● Methods of stock control	6.1	2
● Methods of materials pricing: (see Range Statement)	6.2	2
● Basic analysis of variances: usage, price	6.1, 6.3	9
● Procedures for establishing standard materials costs, use of technical and purchasing information	6.1	8
● Purchasing procedures and documentation	6.1	2, 6
● Methods of analysing materials usage: reasons for wastage	6.1	2, 7, 9
● Procedures for establishing standard labour costs: use of work study information and information about labour rates	6.2	8
● Basic analysis of variances: rate, utilisation	6.2	9

Introduction

ASSESSMENT STRUCTURE

Devolved and central assessment

The units of competence in the AAT Education and Training Scheme are assessed by a combination of devolved assessment and central assessment.

Devolved assessment tests students' ability to apply the skills detailed in the relevant units of competence. Devolved assessment may be carried out by means of:

(a) simulations of workplace activities set by AAT-approved assessors; or
(b) observation in the workplace by AAT-approved assessors.

Central assessments are set and marked by the AAT, and concentrate on testing students' grasp of the knowledge and understanding which underpins units of competence.

The Intermediate Stage

Units of competence at the AAT Intermediate Stage (NVQ/SVQ level 3) are tested by central assessment (CA) and devolved assessment (DA) as follows.

Unit number		Central assessment	Devolved assessment
4	Recording capital transactions	N/A	✓
5	Preparing financial accounts	✓	✓
6*	Recording cost information	✓	✓
7*	Preparing reports and returns	✓	✓
8	Preparing VAT returns	N/A	✓
21	Information technology environment	N/A	✓
22	Using spreadsheets	N/A	✓
25**	Health and safety	N/A	✓

*   From June 1995, there has been a two-hour central assessment for Unit 6 and a two-hour central assessment for Unit 7.

**   If you have already covered Unit 25 Health and Safety at Foundation level you do not need to cover it again. If not, a Health and Safety booklet may be obtained from BPP. (See order form at the back of this text.)

Central Assessment for Unit 6

The central assessment for Unit 6 covers underpinning knowledge and understanding for the Unit. It will consist of some practical problems followed by short-answer questions. All questions and tasks in all parts are to be attempted, none is optional. The time allowed is two hours. Unit 6 has been coded (CA) by the AAT.

BPP MEETS THE AAT

On behalf of students, BPP keeps in touch with the AAT and seeks to determine the approach that should be followed in a central assessment. On this page, we summarise the points in a question and answer form.

Are mark allocations to be provided in a central assessment?

The December 1994 pilot papers were given mark allocations to give guidance on tutors and students as to the proportions of the paper devoted to particular topics. However, the live central assessments will not contain mark allocations, but each section will contain a time allocation.

How much importance do the assessors place on the written elements of the central assessment, as opposed to the numbers?

Candidates must be able to explain the meaning and consequences of calculations made; the importance of understanding the concepts is stressed.

Our understanding is that students should be aware of the Activity Based Costing technique and that no numerical questions would be examined on this topic. Could the assessor confirm this, please?

Activity Based Costing will be assessed either through a case study or a short question.

We understand that students will be assessed on their knowledge and understanding of job, batch and process costing. However, we do not think that students would be assessed on process costing with joint and by-products. Could the assessor confirm this?

An understanding of joint and by-products is necessary but this will only be assessed through the short question section.

Is standard cost bookkeeping assessable i.e. transferring costs to production at standard costs to production and deducing the variances from the 'T' accounts?

Yes.

We understand that students should be able to calculate the following variances : Material - price and usage; Labour - rate, idle time and efficiency; Variable overheads - expenditure and efficiency; Fixed overhead - expenditure, volume and capacity variances. But what about preparing an operating statement reconciling budgeted profit and actual profit?

Such operating statements are considered to be assessable. However, in the current Standards of Competence expenditure and volume variances for overheads are not assessable.

The calculation of Overhead Absorption Rates (OARs) and using a suitable basis to do so, would include:-

- *Per Unit basis*
- *Per Labour hour basis*
- *Per Machine hour basis*
- *Percentage of Direct Material, Direct Labour or Prime Cost*

Can the assessor confirm that all of the above are assessable numerically?

Percentage of Direct Material or Prime Cost would not be assessed numerically. All the other methods detailed are assessable numerically.

Can the assessor clarify the level of knowledge, understanding and technical skills required as regards:-

- Marginal Costing
- Labour Turnover
- Methods of Depreciation.

With regards to labour turnover and methods of depreciation, please see the tasks in Section 1 of the December 1996 Central Assessment. Marginal costing is not considered to be assessable, but element 6.4 of the Standards (accounting principles and theory section) lists:

Effects of changes in capacity levels. Nature and significance of overhead costs: fixed costs and variable costs.

Is Economic Order Quantity (EOQ) numerically assessable? If yes, will the formula be given in the Central Assessment?

Yes and yes.

Part A
Materials, labour and expenses

1 Cost information

This chapter covers the following topics.

1   **Practice makes perfect**

2   **Costs in outline**

3   **Costs in detail**

4   **Why record cost information?**

5   **Product costing**

6   **Functional costs**

7   **Standard costs and variances**

8   **Cost accounting and financial accounting**

---

1 PRACTICE MAKES PERFECT

1.1 Before proceeding, a brief note on how to go about your studies. Cost accounting is a very practical subject: at its heart it is about manipulating numbers. This Tutorial Text tells you how to manipulate the numbers and it also tells you why you might want to do so in different circumstances. Unless you actually practise and see the results for yourself, however, you will not fully appreciate what you are learning.

1.2 It is therefore essential that you have the Workbook that accompanies this Tutorial Text alongside you whenever you are studying and that you stop and practise regularly. The *Cost Information* Workbook contains exercises to illustrate all of the major points in the Text. They will test not only your ability to calculate numbers, but also your understanding of the practical implications of your calculations.

1.3 One of the beauties of the costing aspects of accountancy is that you have total freedom to arrive at the 'answers' and present the information as you please, so long as your presentation communicates its point effectively. This liberty can be, however, also one of the biggest problems: where do you start when you are simply asked to organise a mass of figures into something meaningful? In this respect you have much to learn from practising your own presentation skills by tackling all the exercises in the Workbook and, dare we say, learning from the good examples set by our suggested solutions!

1.4 The remainder of this chapter gives a preview of all of the issues raised by Unit 6. All are covered in more detail in the chapters that follow. If you happen to have studied costing before, you will be aware that, to begin with, we are simplifying certain matters. This is to make sure that the important basic ideas get through. Elaboration will come later. If, later on, you feel you are losing your grip of how the various topics discussed fit in with one another, come back to this chapter and skim through it to refresh your memory.

2 COSTS IN OUTLINE

2.1 Let us suppose that in your hand you have a blue biro which you bought in the newsagent's down the road for 18p. Why does the newsagent charge 18p for it? In other words what does that 18p represent?

2.2 From the newsagent's point of view the cost can be split into two.

Price paid by newsagent to wholesaler	Z
Newsagent's 'mark-up'	$\underline{Y}$
	$\underline{18}$ p

2.3 If the newsagent did not charge more for the biro than he paid for it (Y) there would be no point in him selling it. The mark-up itself can be split into further categories.

Pure profit	X
Amount paid to shop assistants	X
Expenses of owning and operating a shop (rent, electricity, cleaning and so on)	$\underline{X}$
	$\underline{\underline{Y}}$

2.4 The newsagent's 'profit' is the amount he personally needs to live: it is like your salary. Different newsagents have different ideas about this: this is why you might pay 20p for an identical biro if you went into another newsagent's. The shop expenses are amounts that have to be paid, whether or not the newsagent sells you a biro, simply to keep the shop going. Again, if other newsagents have to pay higher rent than our newsagent, this might be reflected in the price of biros.

2.5 The amount paid to the wholesaler can be split in a similar way: there will be a profit element and amounts to cover the costs of running a wholesaling business. There might also be a cost for getting the biro from the wholesaler's premises to the shop and, of course, there will be the amount paid to the manufacturer.

2.6 The majority of the remainder of this Tutorial Text takes the point of view of the manufacturer of products since his costs are the most diverse. If you understand the costing that a manufacturer has to do, you will understand the costing performed by any other sort of business.

3 COSTS IN DETAIL

Production costs

3.1 Look at your biro and consider what it consists of. There is probably a blue plastic cap and a little blue thing that fits into the end, and perhaps a yellow plastic sheath. There is an opaque plastic ink holder with blue ink inside it. At the tip there is a gold plastic part holding a metal nib with a roller ball.

3.2 Let us suppose that the manufacturer sells biros to wholesalers for 5p each. How much does the little ball cost? What share of the 5p is taken up by the little blue thing in the end of the biro? How much did somebody earn for putting it there?

3.3 To elaborate still further, the manufacturer probably has machines to mould the plastic and do some of the assembly. How much does it cost, per biro, to run the machines: to set them up so that they produce the right share of moulded plastic? How much are the production line workers' wages per biro?

3.4 Any of these separate production costs, known as direct costs because they can be traced directly to specific units of production, could be calculated and recorded on a unit cost card which records how the total cost of a unit (in this instance, a pen) is arrived at.

BIRO - UNIT COST CARD		
	£	£
Direct materials		
Yellow plastic	X	
Blue plastic	X	
Opaque plastic	X	
Gold plastic	X	
Ink	X	
Metal	X̲	
		X
Direct labour		
Machine operators' wages	X	
Manual assembly staff wages	X̲	
		X̲
		X
Direct expenses		
Moulding machinery - operating costs	X	
Assembly machinery - operating costs	X̲	
		X̲
Total direct cost (or prime cost)		X
Overheads (production)		X̲
Manufacturing cost (or factory cost)		X̲
Overheads (administration, distribution and selling)		X̲
Total cost		X̲

Cost units

3.5   A cost unit is simply a 'unit' of product which has costs attached to it. The only difficult thing about this is that a cost 'unit' is not always a single item: it might be a batch of 1,000 if that is how the individual items are made. In fact, a cost per 1,000 (or whatever) is often more meaningful information, especially if calculating a cost for a single item gives an amount that you cannot hold in your hand, like 0.003p. Examples of cost units are a construction contract, a batch of 1,000 pair of shoes, a passenger mile (in other words, the transportation of a passenger for a mile) and a patient night (the stay of a patient in hospital for a night).

Cost centres
Centrally assessed 12/96

3.6   'Cost centre' is another important term. A cost centre is something that incurs costs. It might be a place, and this is probably what you think of first because the word 'centre' is often used to mean a place. On the other hand it might be a person: the company solicitor, for example, would incur costs on books and stationery that were unique to his or her function. It might be a group of people, all contributing to the same function: the accounting staff, say, or the laboratory staff. Or it might be an item of equipment: a machine incurs costs because it needs to be oiled and maintained.

3.7   Cost centres may vary in nature, but what they have in common is that they incur costs. It is therefore logical to collect costs initially under the headings of the various different cost centres that there may be in an organisation. Then, when we want to know how much our products cost, we simply find out how many cost units have been produced and share out the costs incurred by that cost centre amongst the cost units.

Overheads

3.8   Overheads (or indirect costs) include costs that go into the making of the biro that you do not see when you dismantle it. You can touch the materials and you can appreciate that a combination of man and machine put them together. It is not so obvious that the manufacturer has had to lubricate machines and employ foremen to supervise the assembly staff. He also has to pay rent for his factory, rent for somewhere to house his stock of materials, someone to buy materials, recruit labour and run the payroll. Other people are paid to deliver the finished biros to the wholesalers; still others are out and about persuading wholesalers to buy biros, and they are supported at head office by staff taking orders and collecting payments.

3.9   In addition certain costs that could be identified with a specific product are classified as overheads and not direct costs. Nails used in the production of a cupboard can be identified specifically with the cupboard. However, because the cost is likely to be relatively insignificant, the expense of tracing such costs does not justify the possible benefits from calculating more accurate direct costs. Instead of keeping complex and time consuming records which might enable us to trace such costs directly to specific units of production, we try to apportion them and other overheads (indirect costs) to each cost unit in as fair a way as possible.

3.10   Overheads are your biggest problem if you are going to be a cost accountant because you cannot easily tell by either looking at or measuring the product, what overheads went into getting it into the hands of the buyer. Overheads, or indirect costs, unlike direct costs, will not be identified with any one product because they are incurred for the benefit of all products rather than for any one specific product.

Make sure that you understand the distinction between direct and indirect costs: it is important.

Direct and indirect costs

3.11 To summarise so far, the cost of an item can be divided into the following cost elements.

(a) Materials
(b) Labour
(c) Expenses

Each element can be split into two, as follows.

Materials	=	Direct materials	+	Indirect materials
+		+		+
Labour	=	Direct labour	+	Indirect labour
+		+		+
Expenses	=	Direct expenses	+	Indirect expenses
Total cost	=	Direct cost		Overhead

Fixed costs and variable costs

3.12 We must mention one other important distinction and that is between fixed costs and variable costs.

(a) If you produce two identical biros you will use twice as many direct materials as you would if you only produced one biro. Direct materials are in this case a *variable* cost. They vary according to the volume of production.

(b) If you oil your machines after every 1,000 biros have been produced, the cost of oil is also a *variable* cost. It is an indirect material cost that varies according to the volume of production.

(c) If you rent the factory that houses your biro-making machines you will pay the same amount of rent per annum whether you produce one biro or 10,000 biros. Factory rental is an indirect expense and it is *fixed* no matter what the volume of activity is.

3.13 The examples in (b) and (c) are both indirect costs, or overheads, but (b) is a variable overhead and (c) is a fixed overhead. The example in (a) is a variable direct cost. Direct costs usually are variable although they do not have to be.

3.14 We are elaborating this point because it can be a source of great confusion. Variable cost is *not* just another name for a direct cost. The distinctions that can be made are as follows.

(a) Costs are either variable or fixed, depending upon whether they change when the volume of production changes.

(b) Costs are either direct or indirect, depending upon how easily they can be traced to a specific unit of production.

4 WHY RECORD COST INFORMATION?

4.1 In case you are beginning to think that recording cost information is far more trouble than it is worth we shall now consider why we bother. There are a number of very good reasons.

Determining the selling price

4.2 In the first place, if an item costs 18p and it is sold for 15p then the seller makes a loss on every sale. Before long he will go out of business. It is therefore important to know how much things cost so that a suitable selling price can be set.

Decision making

4.3 Before deciding on the selling price, the seller had to decide whether to make the item at all. Suppose he could make one or other of two items, either of which could be sold for 15p each. If one cost 10p to make and the other cost 12p then it would be better to make the one that cost 10p. Costing is therefore essential to *decision making*.

Planning and budgeting

4.4 Having decided to make the item it is then necessary to work out the best way of going about it. Sellers are limited as to the number of items they can sell and as to the amount of money they have available to invest in a project. You might conduct market research that told you you could sell 10,000 items,. You would then need cost information so that you could plan what quantity of materials you could afford to buy, how many staff to employ, and how long to keep the machines running each day. Costing is thus an integral part of *planning* for the future.

4.5 Another term for planning of this sort is *budgeting*. You will learn about this at NVQ Level 4. For now you can simply think of a budget as a plan that shows how much money you expect to make and how much it will cost to produce the items (or services) that bring this money in.

Control

4.6 There is, of course, no guarantee that everything will go according to plan. You might make and sell your 10,000 items for 15p each, only to discover that the actual cost of each item had gone up to 18p, perhaps because the suppliers of materials had put their prices up, or because workers had demanded higher wages. Costing is not a one-off exercise. Costs can be predicted in advance but they must also be monitored as they are actually incurred. If this is done then an increase in materials costs, say, can be spotted as soon as it arises and the implications for the future assessed. It may be possible to buy cheaper materials and keep costs down to the level planned or it may be necessary to draw up an entirely new plan. The recording of cost information in such a way that it can be monitored is thus vital to maintain *control of* the business.

Reporting

4.7 Finally, costs have to be recorded so that a business can report its results. Companies have to prepare accounts to comply with the Companies Acts and all businesses need to have some records so that the Inland Revenue knows how much tax is due and Customs and Excise know whether VAT is being properly accounted for. Senior managers judge the performance of their subordinates according to whether they have managed to meet targets which include targets for cost control. Cost information is essential for *reporting*.

5 PRODUCT COSTING

Job costing

5.1 There are several different ways of arriving at a value for the different cost elements (material, labour and expenses) which make up a unit cost of production. The most straightforward case is where the thing to be costed is a one-off item. For example, a furniture maker may make a table, say, to a customer's specific requirements. From start to finish the costs incurred to make that table are identifiable: so much for the table top, so much for the legs, and so on. This form of costing is known as job costing.

2 Materials

This chapter covers the following topics.

1   Types of materials

2   Buying materials

3   Valuing materials issues and stocks

4   Stock control

5   Computers and stock control

6   Reordering stock

7   Direct and indirect materials costs

---

1   TYPES OF MATERIALS

1.1   Although you are expected to know something about 'types of materials', this does not mean that you have to know the chemical formula for materials used in your organisation. It is, however, always helpful to think in concrete terms and so we shall begin this chapter by considering the physical aspects of the things you are going to become adept at costing.

Classifying materials

1.2   There are a number of different ways in which materials can be classified. They can be classified according to the substance that makes them up, for example wood or metal. Many items will be made up of a combination of substances.

1.3   Another way of classifying materials is according to how they are measured. In practice you will very quickly find that materials really come in 'bags' or 'packets' or by the thousand. Moreover, in the UK, imperial measures (feet, inches, pounds, ounces) are still used. When dealing with materials in practice this aspect is something to be very wary of: does the product you are costing need ten individual units (for example kilograms) of material or ten packets, each of which contains one hundred individual units? Obviously this can make a substantial difference to your figures!

1.4   A third way of classifying materials is by one or several of their physical properties such as colour, shape or quality.

Raw materials

1.5   You will frequently come across the term 'raw materials' and what we have described so far may seem to be raw materials. This is, however, a matter of perspective. A headlight assembly is a finished article for a car component manufacturer but for Ford it is one of the 'materials' that make up their vehicles.

1.6   The definition, therefore, of raw materials is 'goods purchased for incorporation into products for sale'.

Work in progress

1.7   Once a headlight is a headlight it does not stop being a headlight simply because it happens to be attached to a Ford Escort. In accounting terms, however, it does change its identity: it becomes part of a car that is in the course of being assembled, that is of 'work in progress'. Work in progress represents an intermediate stage between the manufacturer purchasing the materials that go to make up the car, and the finished Ford Escort. Some work has been done on the materials purchased as part of the process of producing the finished car, but the production process is not complete. Valuing work-in-progress is one of the most difficult tasks in costing. We shall not go into detail here, but just to say although you may know how much it costs to buy a headlight, surely it is worth more once it has been attached to a chassis and wired up. If so, how much more?

Finished goods

1.8   Once the Escort is completed it will be a finished good *ready* for sale or despatch.

2 BUYING MATERIALS

Purchasing procedures

2.1 All businesses have to buy materials of some sort, and this means that decisions have to be made and somebody has to be responsible for doing the buying.

2.2 Large businesses have specialist buying departments managed by people who are very skilled at the job.

2.3 In spite of this, the essence of a buying transaction is simple and, in fact, familiar because you buy things every day and (mainly subconsciously) go through the following process.

(a) You need something.

(b) You find out where you can buy it.

(c) If there is a choice you identify which item is most suitable, taking into account the cost and the quality, and from whom you will buy it.

(d) You order the item, or perhaps several if you will need more in the future.

(e) You receive the item.

(f) You pay for the item.

2.4 In a business this process will be more involved, but only because those spending the money are likely to be different from those looking after the goods and those using them, and because none of those people will actually own the money used. The following diagram illustrates who will be involved.

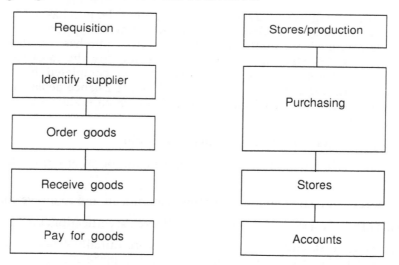

Documentation

2.5 Clearly there needs to be some means by which different departments can let each other know what they want and what is being done about it, and even the smallest business will need to keep records of some sort. We shall describe a manual system that might be used in a fairly large organisation. In reality it is likely that much of the procedure would be computerised, but this does not alter the basic principles or information flows.

Purchase requisition form

2.6 The first stage as the information shows will be that the department requiring the goods will complete a *purchase requisition form* asking the purchasing department to carry out the necessary transaction. An example is shown below. Note that the purchase requisition will usually need some form of authorisation, probably that of a senior person in the department requiring the goods and possibly also that of a senior person in the finance department if substantial expense is involved.

PURCHASE REQUISITION	Req. No.		
Department _____ Suggested Supplier:	Date Requested by: Latest date required:		
Quantity	Description	Estimated Cost	
		Unit	£
Authorised signature:			

Order form

2.7 Often the business will use a regular source of supply. The purchasing department may, however, be aware of special offers or have details of new suppliers: part of its job is to keep up to date with what is on the market. Thus once a purchase requisition is received in the purchasing department, the first task is to identify the most suitable supplier. Whatever the decision made, an *order form* is then completed by the purchasing department (again, it may have to be authorised by the finance department) and this is sent to the supplier. The order form, an example of which is shown below, will contain the following details.

(a) The name and address of the ordering organisation

(b) The date of order, and reference numbers for both ordering department and supplier

(c) The address and date(s) for delivery (by road, rail, air and so on) or collection

(d) Details of goods/services: quantity, code (if any), specification, unit costs and so on

An order form should be sent even if goods are initially ordered by telephone, to confirm that the order is a legitimate one and to make sure that the supplier does not overlook it.

Purchase Order/Confirmation		Albert Hall Instruments Southern Cross Trading Estate Bognor Regis West Sussex		

Our Order Ref: Date

To

⌜*(Address)*   ⌝   Please deliver to the above address

Ordered by:

Passed and checked by:

L   ⌟   Total Order Value £

		Subtotal	
		VAT (@ 17.5%)	
		Total	

2.8   The purchase order is important because it provides a means by which the business can later check that the goods received are the same as those ordered. Copies can be sent to the person who requisitioned the goods so that he knows they are on their way and also to the stores so that they can arrange to accommodate the goods. Either now or later a copy can be sent to the accounts department so that they can see that goods invoiced were genuinely required and that the purchase was properly authorised.

Despatch note

2.9   Certain other documents may arise before the goods are actually received. The supplier may acknowledge the order and perhaps indicate how long it is likely to take to be fulfilled. A *despatch note* may be sent to warn that the goods are on their way.

Delivery note

2.10 We now move to the stores department. When the goods are delivered, goods inwards will be presented with a *delivery note* or *advice note* (although bear in mind that smaller suppliers may not go to these lengths). This is the supplier's document (a copy is signed by the person receiving the goods and returned to the supplier) and, as such, there is no guarantee that its details are correct. If the actual goods cannot be inspected immediately, the delivery note should be signed 'subject to inspection'.

Goods received note

2.11 Once the goods have been delivered they should be inspected as soon as possible. A *goods received note (GRN)* will be completed by goods inwards on the basis of a physical check, which involves counting the items received and seeing that they are not damaged.

```
                                              ACCOUNTS COPY

       GOODS RECEIVED NOTE WAREHOUSE COPY

   DATE: ___7 March 19X5___   TIME: ___2.00 pm___      NO  5565

   ORDER NO: _____

   SUPPLIER'S ADVICE NOTE NO: _____   WAREHOUSE A

   ┌─────────────┬──────────────┬────────────────────────────────┐
   │  QUANTITY   │   CAT NO     │  DESCRIPTION                   │
   ├─────────────┼──────────────┼────────────────────────────────┤
   │             │              │                                │
   │     16      │   SR 424     │  Granular salt, 25kg bags      │
   │             │              │                                │
   │             │              │                                │
   │             │              │                                │
   │             │              │                                │
   ├─────────────┴──────────────┴────────────────────────────────┤
   │ RECEIVED IN GOOD CONDITION:     F. P.          (INITIALS)    │
   └──────────────────────────────────────────────────────────────┘
```

2.12 A copy of the GRN can be sent to the purchasing department so that it can be matched with the purchase order. This is to make sure that the correct number and specification of items have been received. Any discrepancies would be taken up with the supplier.

2.13 A copy of the GRN would also be sent to the accounts department so that it can be matched with the *invoice* when it is received. The payment of the invoice is the end of the transaction (unless there is a mistake on the invoice or there was some problem with the delivery, in which case a *credit note* may later be received from the supplier).

Buying and costing

2.14 Clearly the buying department needs to retain cost information for the purpose of identifying suitable suppliers. This is likely to be in the form of catalogues and price lists. From the point of view of costing products such information will be useful when new products are being assessed and when setting standard costs for materials (see later).

2.15 The costing department is, however, chiefly interested in the actual cost of materials as shown on the *invoice* and included in the accounting records as cash and credit transactions.

Example: Buying and costing

2.16 It is Guy Hook's first day in the costing department and he has been told to calculate the materials cost of job 7654 which has just been completed. No invoice has yet been received for the main material used, which is known as XK50. Guy uses his initiative and pops down to the purchasing department to see if they can help. They are rather busy but someone hands him a very well-thumbed catalogue and a thick file of purchase orders, all relating to the supplier of XK50. There are many orders for XK50, one of which has today's date. How should Guy go about costing the XK50 used for job 7654?

Solution: Buying and costing

2.17 The quickest thing to do would be to phone up the supplier and ask what price will be charged for the order in question, but there might be good reasons for not doing this (for example not wishing to prompt an earlier invoice than usual!) It seems likely that, in the absence of the actual information, the best way of ascertaining a price for XK50 is to consult the catalogue (assuming it is up to date) and to find the most recent purchase order that *has* been invoiced. If there is a discrepancy, previous invoices could be looked at to see if they show a price rise since the date of the catalogue. If the price fluctuates widely it might be better to calculate an average.

2.18 As Guy gets to know his way around the system he will learn which are the most reliable sources of information. Possibly some suppliers make frequent errors on invoices but quote correct unit prices on delivery notes. The moral is: always be on your guard for errors.

3 VALUING MATERIALS ISSUES AND STOCKS
Centrally assessed 6/95 - 6/97

Just-in-time stock policy

3.1 The implicit assumption in the Guy Hook example above was that materials were bought specifically for individual jobs and therefore that each order could be identified with a particular job. This is possible in practice. Certainly, keeping large quantities of stock is something to be avoided in the 1990s business environment. Holding stock means that you have to have somewhere to put it and so it takes up space that could be used for other purposes. Often it means employing somebody to look after it, perhaps 24 hours a day if it is very valuable.

3.2 Ideally, you should receive an order for so many items of the product in question, buy exactly the right quantity of materials to make that many items and be left with no stocks of finished goods, work in progress or raw materials. This is known as the just-in-time (JIT) approach: just-in-time purchasing of stocks to meet just-in-time production of goods ordered. From the point of view of costing, there is very little difficulty with the JIT approach. The materials costs of each production run are known because the materials used were bought specially for that run. There was no stock to start with and there is none left over.

Buffer stock

3.3 However the approach that is more common in practice is to keep a certain amount of stock in reserve to cope with fluctuations in demand and with suppliers who cannot be relied upon to deliver the right quality and quantity of materials at the right time. This reserve of stock is known as *buffer stock*. The valuation of buffer stock is one of the most important elements of your studies at this level.

Example

3.4 Suppose, for example, that you have 50 litres of a chemical in stock. You buy 2,000 litres to allow for the next batch of production. Both the opening stock and the newly-purchased stock cost £2 per litre.

	Litres	£
Opening stock	50	100
Purchases	2,000	4,000
	2,050	4,100

3.5 You actually use 1,600 litres, leaving you with 450 litres. You know that each of the 1,600 litres used cost £2, as did each of the 450 litres remaining. There is no costing problem here.

3.6 Now suppose that in the following month you decide to buy 1,300 litres, but have to pay £2.10 per litre because you lose a 10p discount if buying under 1,500 litres.

	Litres	Cost per litre £	Total cost £
Opening stock	450	2.00	900
Purchases	1,300	2.10	2,730
	1,750		3,630

For the next batch of production you use 1,600 litres, as before. What did the 1,600 litres used cost, and what value should you give to the 150 litres remaining?

3.7 If we could identify which litres were used there would be no problem. Some would cost £2 per litre but most would cost £2.10. It may not, however, be possible to identify litres used. For instance, the chemical may not be perishable, and new purchases be simply mixed in with older stock in a central tank. There would thus be no way of knowing which delivery the 1,600 litres used belonged to. Even if the chemical were stored in tins with date stamps it would be a tedious chore to keep track of precisely which tins were used when (and since they are all the same, the exercise has no virtue from the point of view of the quality of the final product.)

3.8 It may not therefore be possible or desirable to track the progress of each individual litre. However we need to know:

(a) the cost of the litres that we have used so that we know how much to charge for the final product and so that we can compare this cost with the equivalent cost in earlier or future periods;

(b) the cost of closing stock both because it will form part of the usage figure in the next period and for financial accounting purposes. Closing stock is often a significant figure in the financial statements and it appears in both the profit and loss account and the balance sheet.

3.9 We therefore have to use a consistent method of pricing the litres which provides a reasonable approximation of the costs of the stock. Possible methods of valuing stock are:

(a) *FIFO-first in, first out*

This method values issues at the prices of the oldest items in stock at the time the issues were made. The remaining stock will thus be valued at the price of the most recent purchases. Say, for example stock consisted of four deliveries in the last month:

	Units		
1 May	1,000	at	£2.00
8 May	500	at	£2.50
15 May	500	at	£3.00
22 May	1,000	at	£3.50

If on 23 May 1,500 units were issued, 1,000 of these units would be priced at £2 (the cost of the 1,000 oldest units in stock), 500 at £2.50 (the cost of the next oldest 500). 1,000 units of closing stock would be valued at £3.50 (the cost of the 1,000 most recent units received) 500 units at £3.00 (the cost of the next most recent 500).

(b) *LIFO - Last in, first out*

This method is the opposite of FIFO. Issues will be valued at the prices of the most recent purchases; hence stock remaining will be valued at the cost of the oldest items. In the example in (a) it will be 1,000 units of *issues* which will be valued at £3.50, and the other 500 units issued will be valued at £3.00. 1,000 units of *closing stock* will be valued at £2.00, and 500 at £2.50.

(c) *Cumulative weighted average pricing*

With this method we calculate an average cost of all the litres in stock whenever a new delivery is received. Thus the individual price of the units issued *and* of the units in closing stock will be:

$$\frac{\text{Total cost of units in stock at 22 May}}{\text{Units in stock at 22 May}}$$

22 May being the date of the last delivery

The average price per unit will be $\frac{8,250}{3,000}$ equals £2.75.

(d) *Replacement cost*

This method values issues and stock at the cost to the business of replacing that stock. Replacement cost enables the business to see quickly what resources will be required to replace its assets.

(e) *Standard cost*

This method is covered in Chapter 8.

3.10 Further examples of how FIFO, LIFO and cumulative weighted average pricing work in practice are given below. Say a business has opening stock of 450 litres valued at £2 per litre, buys 1,300 litres at £2.10 and uses 1,600 litres. What will be the cost of usage and value of closing stock?

(a) *FIFO*

	Litres	Cost £	£
Opening stock	450	2.00	900
Purchases	1,300	2.10	2,730
	1,750		3,630
Usage (Opening stock)	(450)	2.00	(900)
	1,300		2,730
Usage (1,600 – 450) (Purchases)	(1,150)	2.10	(2,415)
Closing stock	150		315

Total cost of usage is £900 + £2,415 = £3,315 and the value of closing stock is £315.

(b) *LIFO*

	Litres	Cost £	£
Opening stock	450	2.00	900
Purchases	1,300	2.10	2,730
	1,750		3,630
Usage (Purchases)	(1,300)	2.10	(2,730)
	450		900
Usage (1,600 – 1,300) (Opening stock)	(300)	2.00	(600)
	150		300

Total cost of usage is £2,730 + £600 = £3,330 and the value of closing stock is £300.

(c)   *Cumulative weighted average pricing*

	Litres	Cost £	£
Opening stock	450	2.000	900
Purchases	1,300	2.100	2,730
Stock at (£3,630/1,750)	1,750	2.074	3,630
Usage	(1,600)	2.074	(3,318)
	150		312

Usage costs £3,318 under this method and closing stock is valued at £312.

3.11   Note that the total of usage costs plus closing stock value is the same (£3,630) whichever method is used. In other words, the total expenditure of £3,630 is simply split between the expenses for the period and the remaining asset (stock) value in different proportions. The total expense will eventually be charged as usage costs but, according to the method used, different amounts will be charged in different periods.

3.12   The different results in these examples are not very marked because we are dealing with fairly small quantities and the price fluctuation was not very significant. Imagine if we had been dealing in hundreds of thousands of litres or that the cost of the chemical had gone up by 50p: the differences would be, as you can imagine, far more significant.

Which method is correct?

3.13   This is a trick question because there is no one correct method. Each has advantages and disadvantages and the choice therefore depends upon the significance that an organisation attaches to specific arguments.

Features of FIFO

3.14   FIFO may represent what is actually happening; it is quite likely that the oldest stock is used first. However, FIFO is not necessarily very helpful to production managers. During periods of rising prices, if stocks are quite old they may be issued to production at a cost which is considerably less than what it now costs to replace them. If production managers believe a material is cheaper than it really is they may be more liberal than they should be in their use of it.

Features of LIFO

3.15   LIFO avoids the above problem; stocks are issued to production at a cost which is close to current market value. Closing stock values will, however, be significantly understated since older stock, which 'makes up' the closing stock, will have cost less than the current market value.

Features of weighted average pricing

3.16   Weighted average pricing is a compromise between FIFO and LIFO, but it rarely represents an actual price that could be found in the market. However, the calculations are less cumbersome with weighted average pricing because there is no need to identify each batch separately. With both FIFO and LIFO records must be kept of the issue of each batch purchased. If for example, in 3.10(a) 400 litres had been issued, and not 450, the stock records would have to show that the balance remaining in stock was 50 litres at £2.00 and 1,300 at £2.10.

Features of replacement cost

3.17   The main problem with replacement cost is keeping track of price changes. In the example in 3.10 above, if the chemical actually cost £2.20 per litre on the day the 1,600 litres were used, the cost of production would be £3,520 and the value of closing stock would be £330. Suppose, however, that the market price was £2.18 on the next day. Issues on that day would be valued at £2.18, likewise remaining stock. Suppose then price changed again, to £2.24 on the day after that: you can probably feel the administrative headache coming on just thinking about it. Replacement cost is therefore not much used in practice. A LIFO approach is a pretty good approximation if replacement information is wanted.

3.18 The final point that must be remembered is that the pricing decisions under FIFO and LIFO do not affect what items of stock are *actually* issued. A business may, for example, adopt a FIFO pricing policy, but the storekeeper issue the items required out of stock entirely at random.

3.19 The financial accounting aspects of FIFO and LIFO are covered in units 4 and 5 of your studies.

4 STOCK CONTROL

4.1 Stock control is the *regulation* of stock levels, one aspect of which is putting a value to the amounts of stock issued and remaining, as described above. The stock control system can also be said to include ordering, purchasing and receiving goods and keeping track of them while they are in the warehouse.

This section deals with the location of stock. Section 5 deals with using computers to control stocks; Section 6 deals with the other aspect of stock control, namely reordering decisions.

Locating stock

4.2 In a previous section we left our stock at the door of the warehouse, while we completed a goods received note. It is now time to see what happens before it is actually used.

4.3 You can probably picture a warehouse - a large room with rows and rows of high shelving, perhaps moveable ladders and maybe barrows or fork-lift trucks. Very modern 'highbay' warehouses have automatic guided vehicles (AGVs), stacker cranes and conveyors, all controlled by computer. All of this implies organisation: when they are brought into the warehouse stocks are not simply dumped in the nearest available space. There is a place for everything and everything is in its place. There is no point in keeping stock at all if you don't know where to find it when it is needed.

4.4 Suppose, for example, that a warehouse were arranged as shown below, A to F representing rows of shelving and 1 to 7 the access bays between them. Suppose the shelves were 4m high, 10m long and 1m wide and you needed to locate five 10 mm washers in stainless steel. (To put it another way, suppose you had a haystack and you were looking for a needle!) How would you go about organising the warehouse so that you could always find what you were looking for?

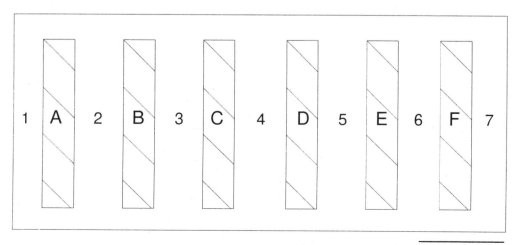

4.5   The solution is fairly obvious. You need to divide up the shelf-racks and give each section a code. A typical warehouse might organise its shelving as shown below.

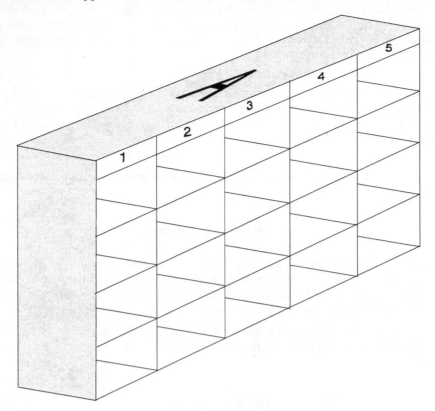

4.6   You also need to keep a record which shows the whereabouts in the warehouse of all the different types of stock, including the 10mm washers in stainless steel. Suppose that the washers are listed as being kept in location A234. The reference A234 would take you to Row A, bay 2, bin 3, shelf 4. Shelf 4 might contain a series of drawers containing washers of various sizes, each drawer being labelled with a precise part number (A234/1279, say) and a description of the item. (Coding is discussed in more detail below.)

4.7   '*Bin*' simply means a receptacle: in warehouse terms it normally means a division of shelving (or simply one shelf) or some other container which can be located by a code letter or number. The term is in general usage but it does not have a precise meaning.

4.8   In the light of this you should understand what a *bin card* is. In a manual system the bin card is kept *with the actual stock* and is updated whenever items are removed or added to provide an accurate record of the quantity in stock for each stores item. (Maximum, minimum and reorder level will be explained later in the chapter.)

```
                          BIN  CARD

    Description ...............................   Bin No: ...........................
                 ..............................   Code No:...........................
    Normal Quantity to order.................    Maximum:...........................
                                                  Minimum:...........................
                                                  Re-order Level: ...................
```

Receipts			Issues			Balance	Remarks
Date	G.R.N No.	Quantity	Date	Req. No.	Quantity	Quantity	

Note that the bin card does not need to show any information about the cost of materials.

4.9   Organisations will also maintain what are known as *stores ledger accounts*, an example of an account being shown below.

STORES LEDGER ACCOUNT

Material: ....   Maximum Quantity: ....

Code: ....   Minimum Quantity: ....

Date	Receipts				Issues				Stock		
	G.R.N. No.	Quantity	Unit Price £	Amount £	Stores Req. No.	Quantity	Unit Price £	Amount £	Quantity	Unit Price £	Amount £

Details from GRNs and materials requisition notes (see later) are used to update stores ledger accounts, which then provide a record of the quantity and value of each line of stock in the stores. The stores ledger accounts are normally kept in the cost department or in the stores office whereas the bin cards are written up and actually kept in the stores. There are two advantages to this procedure.

(a)   The accounting records can be maintained more accurately and in a better condition by a cost clerk or an experienced stores clerk than by a stores assistant.

(b)   A control check is provided. The balances on the bin cards in the stores can be compared with the balances on the stores ledger accounts.

4.10   Stores ledger accounts are very much like the individual accounts in the debtors and creditors ledger. They are memorandum accounts, the aggregate of their monetary value equalling the balance on the stock control account (just as the aggregate of the balances on the creditors ledger equals the balance on the creditors ledger control account). The stock control account is the stock account in the nominal ledger.

4.11 The use of bin cards and stores ledger accounts ensures that every issue and receipt of stock is recorded as it occurs so that there is a continuous clerical record of the balance of each item of stock. This is known as a *perpetual inventory system*.

4.12 You may be thinking that the system we have described is rather over-complicated. Why not, for example, start at one end of the room and end at the other numbering each separate location in sequence and numbering each stock item accordingly? The reasons are for practicality and flexibility. If item 1 is a 10mm washer and item 2 is an exhaust pipe they are hardly going to fit into the same size drawer. If item 1 is a 10mm washer and item 2 is a 15mm washer, what happens when a new product needs 12mm washers? If item 1 is used twice a year and item 10,001 is used every day the storekeeper will be collapsing with exhaustion by the end of the day if item 1 is the one nearest the issue point. If item 1 is a large heavy item and item 10,001 is also a large heavy item the storeman will be driving the fork-lift from one end of the warehouse to the other all day. It is therefore far better to have large heavy items in close proximity and to have frequently used items near to the issue point.

4.13 The last point is worth developing a little. Storekeeping involves a good deal of commonsense and a considerable knowledge of the types of stock held, and an effective storekeeping system should take the following points into account.

(a) Heavy items should not be stored on high shelves (in case the shelves collapse and to make handling as safe and unstrenuous as possible).

(b) Dangerous items (for example items with sharp edges) should not be stored above eye level.

(c) Items liable to be damaged by flood (for example paper stock) should not be stored on low shelves.

(d) Special arrangements should be made for the storage and handling of chemicals and flammable materials.

(e) Some stocks are sensitive to temperature and should be stored accordingly.

(f) Other stocks may have special hygiene or 'clean air' requirements.

Coding of materials

4.14 Each item held in stores must be unambiguously identified and this can best be done by numbering them with stock codes. The advantages of this are as follows.

(a) Ambiguity is avoided. Different people may use different descriptions for materials. This is avoided if numbers are used.

(b) Time is saved. Descriptions can be lengthy and time-consuming, particularly when completing written forms.

(c) Production efficiency is improved. If the correct material can be accurately identified from a code number, production hold-ups caused by the issue of incorrect material can be avoided.

(d) Computerised processing is made easier.

(e) Numbered code systems can be designed to be flexible, and can be expanded to include more stock items as necessary.

The digits in a code can stand for the type of stock, supplier, location and so forth. For example stock item A234/1279 might refer to the item of stock kept in row A, bay 2, bin 3, shelf 4. The item might be identified by the digits 12 and its supplier might be identified by the digits 79.

Issuing materials

4.15 The sole point of holding stocks is so that they can be used to make products. This means that they have to be issued from stores to production. This transaction will be initiated by production who will complete a *materials requisition note* and pass it to the warehouse.

```
+-----------------------------------------------------------------------+
|                      MATERIALS REQUISITION                            |
|   Material Required for:                               No.            |
|      (Job or Overhead Account)                                        |
|   Department:                              Date:                      |
+----------+-------------+--------+--------+--------+--------+-----------+
|          |             | Code   |        |        |        |           |
| Quantity | Description | No.    | Weight | Rate   |  £     |  Notes    |
+----------+-------------+--------+--------+--------+--------+-----------+
|          |             |        |        |        |        |           |
|          |             |        |        |        |        |           |
|          |             |        |        |        |        |           |
|          |             |        |        |        |        |           |
+----------+-------------+--------+--------+--------+--------+-----------+
|   Foreman:                                                            |
+-----------------------------------------------------------------------+
```

4.16 The stores department will locate the stock, withdraw the amount required and update the bin card as appropriate. The stores ledger account will also be updated.

4.17 If the amount of materials required is overestimated the excess should be put back into store accompanied by a *materials returned note*. The form in our illustration is almost identical to a requisition note. In practice it would be wise to colour code the two documents (one white, one yellow, say) to prevent confusion.

```
+-----------------------------------------------------------------------+
|                      MATERIALS RETURNED NOTE                          |
|   Material not needed for:                             No.            |
|      (Job or Overhead Account)                                        |
|   Department:                              Date:                      |
+----------+-------------+--------+--------+--------+--------+-----------+
|          |             | Code   |        |        |        |           |
| Quantity | Description | No.    | Weight | Rate   |  £     |  Notes    |
+----------+-------------+--------+--------+--------+--------+-----------+
|          |             |        |        |        |        |           |
|          |             |        |        |        |        |           |
|          |             |        |        |        |        |           |
|          |             |        |        |        |        |           |
+----------+-------------+--------+--------+--------+--------+-----------+
|   Foreman:                                                            |
+-----------------------------------------------------------------------+
```

4.18 There may be occasions when materials already issued but not required for one job can be used for another job in progress. In this case there is no point in returning the materials to the warehouse. Instead a *materials transfer note* can be raised. This prevents one job being charged with too many materials and another with too little.

4.19 You will note that all of the forms shown above have spaces for cost information (that is, monetary values). This will be inserted either by the stores department or in costing, depending upon how the system is organised. We have already described the various bases which may be used to put a value on stock - FIFO, LIFO or an average figure.

Stocktaking
Centrally assessed 6/96

4.20 Stocktaking involves counting the physical stock on hand at a certain date and then checking this against the balance shown in the clerical records. There are two methods of carrying out this process.

(a) *Periodic stocktaking*. This is usually carried out annually and the objective is to count all items of stock on a specific date.

(b) *Continuous stocktaking*. This involves counting and checking a number of stock items on a regular basis so that each item is checked at least once a year, and valuable items can be checked more frequently. This has a number of advantages over periodic stocktaking. It is less disruptive, less prone to error, and achieves greater control.

Stock discrepancies

4.21 There will be occasions when stock checks disclose discrepancies between the physical amount of an item in stock and the amount shown in the stock records. When this occurs, the cause of the discrepancy should be investigated, and appropriate action taken to ensure that it does not happen again. Possible causes of discrepancies are as follows.

(a) Suppliers deliver a different quantity of goods than is shown on the goods received note. Since this note is used to update stock records, a discrepancy will arise. This can be avoided by ensuring that all stock is counted as it is received, and a responsible person should sign the document to verify the quantity.

(b) The quantity of stock issued to production is different from that shown on the materials requisition note. Careful counting of all issues will prevent this.

(c) Excess stock is returned from production without documentation. This can be avoided by ensuring that all movements of stock are accurately documented - in this case, a materials returned note should be raised.

(d) Clerical errors may occur in the stock records. Regular checks by independent staff should detect and correct mistakes.

(e) Breakages in stores may go unrecorded. All breakages should be documented and noted on the stock records.

(f) Employees may steal stock. Regular checks or continuous stocktaking will help to prevent this, and only authorised personnel should be allowed into the stores.

4.22 If the stock discrepancy is found to be caused by clerical error, then the records should be rectified immediately. If the discrepancy occurs because units of stock appear to be missing, the lost stock must be written off. If actual stock is greater than recorded stock, extra units of stock are added to the stock records. The accounting transaction will be recorded by a stores credit note, where items of stock have been lost, or a stores debit note, when there is more actual stock than recorded.

4.23 A stores credit note may have the following format.

STORES CREDIT NOTE			
Quantity	Item code	Description	£

Continuous stocktaking report number..

Credit note authorised by..

Date ....

5 COMPUTERS AND STOCK CONTROL
Centrally assessed 6/95

5.1 Although the basic principles of stock control are not difficult in themselves, you will appreciate by now that an effective system requires a good deal of administrative effort, even if only a few items of stock are involved. There is therefore a good deal to be gained from computerisation of this function.

Computerised stock files

5.2 A typical computerised stock file would contain a record for each item, each record having fields as follows.

(a) *Stock code:* a unique stock code to identify each item. This could be in bar code form for large organisations.

(b) *Description:* a brief description is helpful when perusing stock records and probably essential when printing out lists of stock for stock-taking purposes. Ideally the system will generate purchase orders which also require brief narrative details.

(c) *Supplier code:* this would match the code for the supplier in the purchase ledger.

(d) *Supplier's reference number:* again this information would be needed for purchase orders.

(e) *Quantity per unit:* this would specify how many individual items there were per 'unit'. This is sometimes called the 'factor'.

(f) *Cost price per item.*

(g) *Control levels:* there would be a field for each of the four control levels (minimum and maximum stock, reorder level and reorder quantity).

(h) *Location:* a location code could be included if it were not part of the stock code itself.

(i) *Movements history:* there could be fields for issues per day, per week, during the last month, in the last year and so on.

(j) *Job code:* there might be a field allowing costs to be linked to specific jobs. Stocks could be 'reserved' for jobs due to be started in the next week, say.

Stock reports

5.3 Before you read on see if you can make your own list of the sort of reports that a system with fields such as those above might be able to generate.

(a) *Daily listing:* a daily list of all items ordered, received, issued or placed on reserve. This might have 'exception reports' for unusual movements of stock and for items that had reached the reorder level.

(b) *Stock lists:* lists could be produced for stocktaking purposes, with stock codes, descriptions and locations. This could be restricted to certain types of stock, such as high value items or stocks with high turnover.

(c) *Stock movements:* a report of stock movements over time would help in setting control levels and in identifying 'slow-moving stock' that is not really required.

(d) *Stock valuations:* this would show current balances and place a value on stocks according to which calculation method (FIFO, LIFO, and so on) was in use.

(e) *Supplier analysis:* this would list all the items of stock purchased from the same supplier, and might be useful for placing orders (several items could be ordered at the same time, cutting delivery costs).

Bill of materials

5.4 Many computerised stock control systems have a 'bill of materials' facility. This allows assembly records (sometimes called 'explosion records') to be compiled, containing details of the various 'assemblies' that make up the final product. A tape deck, for example may have three main assemblies - the motor mechanism, the electronics and the outer casing.

5.5 Each individual assembly could be further broken down into its constituent materials and components.

A common fallacy

5.6 It is sometimes assumed that computerising stock records will guarantee they are 100% accurate. In fact the discrepancies listed in Section 4 are just as likely to occur in a computerised as a non-computerised system. Stocktaking is thus equally important in a computerised stock system as it is in a manual system.

6 REORDERING STOCK
Centrally assessed 6/95 - 6/97

6.1 As noted earlier, the ideal is for businesses not to have any stocks on the premises unless they are about to be used in production which can be sold immediately. In practice many businesses would regard this approach as too risky or impractical because they are unable to predict either their own levels of demand or the reliability of their suppliers or both. They therefore set various 'control levels', the purpose of which is to ensure the following.

(a) The business does not run out of stock and suffer disruption to production as a result. In other words the business needs a certain amount of stock (the *buffer stock)* to guard against unexpected events such as a large increase in demand or suppliers failing to deliver.

(b) The business does not carry an excessive amount of stocks which take up space, incur storage costs and possibly deteriorate with age.

6.2 The problems of when to reorder stock and how much to reorder are the most significant practical problems in stock management. To illustrate the problems in detail and the way in which they may be solved, we shall consider an example.

Example: Stock control levels

6.3 A new manufacturing business is being set up to make a single product. The product is to be made by moulding plastic. Joe, the manager, expects to make 10 units per day and has found that each unit will require 5kg of plastic. He decides to obtain enough materials to last a week (5 days). How much should he order?

6.4 This is not difficult. Joe should order 5 days × 10 units × 5kg = 250kg.

The materials are placed in the stores ready for the commencement of production on the following Monday.

6.5 The following week everything goes as planned, causing great celebration over the weekend. The following Monday however, Joe realises that he has no materials left. (This is called a 'stock-out'). He rings up a number of suppliers but to his dismay none can deliver in less than 2 days. There is therefore no production for the whole of Monday and Tuesday.

6.6 Joe doesn't want this to happen again so he orders four weeks worth of materials, even though this means increasing his overdraft at the bank by £4,000. The materials duly arrive on Wednesday morning but of the 1,000kg delivered (20 × 10 × 5 = 1,000) Joe finds he only has room to store 500kg. To accommodate the remainder he has to rent space in the factory next door at a cost of £20.

6.7 Twenty days go by and production goes as planned. Joe doesn't want to get caught out again, so two days before he is due to run out of materials he places a fresh order, this time for only 500kg.

6.8 Unfortunately, this time the suppliers are unable to deliver in 2 days as promised, but take 4 days. Another 2 days production is lost.

6.9 As Joe's product establishes itself in the market demand starts to increase. He starts to produce 15 units a day but again he is caught out because, obviously, this means that the materials are used up more quickly. He often runs out before the next delivery has arrived.

6.10 So it goes on for the whole of Joe's first year in business. By the end of this time he works out that he has lost nearly three weeks production due to materials shortages. In despair he contacts a management consultant for advice.

Solution: Stock control levels

6.11 Joe is told to calculate a number of figures from his records.

(a) The maximum daily usage

(b) The maximum lead time. (*Lead time* is the time it takes between ordering stocks and having them delivered.)

(c) The average daily usage

(d) The average lead time

(e) The minimum daily usage and minimum lead time

(f) The cost of holding one unit of stock for one year (holding cost)

(g) The cost of ordering a consignment of stock

(h) The annual demand for materials

6.12 Joe has kept careful records and some of these figures cause him little bother.

Maximum usage	100kg per day
Average usage	75kg per day
Minimum usage	50kg per day
Annual demand	19,500kg (52 × 5 × 75kg)

Maximum lead time	4 days
Average lead time	3 days
Minimum lead time	2 days

6.13 The calculation of the *holding cost* is quite complicated. Joe has to work out a number of figures.

   (a)   Materials can only be bought in 5kg boxes and therefore 'one unit' of stock is 5kg, not 1kg.

   (b)   The total cost of having one box in stock is made up of a number of separate costs.

       (i)   Interest paid on the money borrowed to buy one box

       (ii)   Rental of the floor space taken up by one box

       (iii)   The warehouse keeper's wages

       (iv)   Administrative costs of taking deliveries, issuing materials, and keeping track of them

       (v)   The cost of insuring the stock

       Eventually Joe works out that the figure is £0.62 per 'unit' of 5kg. He is shocked by this and wonders whether he should order smaller quantities more frequently. (Fortunately for Joe, there is little risk of obsolescence or deterioration of boxes. Many organisations have to include the cost of obsolescence or deterioration in holding costs, however.)

6.14 *Ordering costs* are also quite difficult to calculate. Joe has to take into account:

   (a)   the cost of stationery and postage;
   (b)   the cost of phoning round to suppliers; and
   (c)   the time taken up by doing this.

He is surprised to find that the figure works out to £19.87 per order and now wonders whether he should make fewer larger orders to keep these costs down.

6.15 Now that Joe has these figures the consultant tells him how to calculate four stock control levels that will help him to avoid running out of stock and to keep down the costs of holding and ordering stock.

   (a)   *Reorder level*. Joe already realises that stocks have to be reordered before they run out completely. This number tells him how low stocks can be allowed to fall before an order should be placed. It assumes that maximum usage and maximum lead time, the two worst events from the point of view of stock control, coincide.

Reorder level   = maximum usage × maximum lead time
                    = 100kg × 4 days
                    = 400kg

   (b)   *Reorder quantity*. Joe has never known what the best amount to order would be. He is beginning to understand that there must be some way of juggling the costs of holding stock, the costs of ordering stock and the amount of stock needed but he does not know how to work it out. His consultant fortunately does and she gives him the following formula.

$$Q = \sqrt{\frac{2cd}{h}}$$

where   h   is the cost of holding one unit of stock for one year
         c   is the cost of ordering a consignment
         d   is the annual demand
         Q   is the 'economic order quantity' (EOQ), that is, the best amount to order

Remembering that a 'unit' of stock is 5kg and therefore annual demand is 19,500kg/5kg = 3,900 units, we can calculate the reorder quantity as follows.

$$Q = \sqrt{\frac{2 \times 19.87 \times 3,900}{0.62}}$$

= 500 units (approximately)
= 2,500kg

6.16 Joe is not entirely convinced by the EOQ calculation but promises to try it out since it seems like a reasonable amount to order. He then asks what the other two control levels are, since he seems to have all the information he needs already. The consultant points out that the calculations done so far don't allow for other uncertain factors like a severe shortage of supply or unexpected rises or falls in demand. As a precaution Joe needs a *minimum stock level* below which stocks should never be allowed to fall, and a *maximum stock level* above which stock should not be able to rise. There is a risk of stock-outs if stock falls below the minimum level and a risk of stock being at a wasteful level if above the maximum level.

Minimum level	= reorder level – (average usage × average lead time)
	= 400kg – (75kg × 3 days)
	= 175kg
Maximum level	= reorder level + reorder quantity –
	(minimum usage × minimum lead time)
	= 400kg + 2,500kg – (50kg × 2 days)
	= 2,800kg

6.17 The story has a happy ending. Joe finds that the EOQ works very well in practice. His costs are reduced and he suffers no stock-outs in the following year. The derivation of the EOQ formula is quite complicated and we suggest that you, too, simply accept it.

6.18 An easier way of working out a reorder quantity is to take the reorder level (400 kg for Joe) and assume that the usage and the lead time will be as little or short as possible. This means that if an order is placed when stock levels reach reorder level, by the time the next delivery is received Joe would have 400 – (2 days × 50 kg) = 300 kg in stock. The quantity to be delivered must not be so much that it takes stock over the maximum level (2,800 kg). The *maximum* reorder quantity in Joe's case is therefore 2,500 kg. This happens to coincide with the economic order quantity, although it need not do so.

7 DIRECT AND INDIRECT MATERIALS COSTS
Centrally assessed 6/95

7.1 To remind you, a direct cost is one that can be traced directly to a product and an indirect cost is one that cannot be traced directly to a product or which it is not worth the trouble of tracing directly to a product.

7.2 All materials becoming part of the product are direct materials unless they are used in negligible amounts and have negligible costs. Examples are as follows.

(a) Materials or parts specially purchased for a particular job, batch or process.

(b) Materials passing from one operation to another. For example if a product is made in two departments, part-finished work transferred from one department to the next becomes finished work of department 1 and a direct material cost in department 2.

(c) Packing materials like cartons and boxes are also often treated as direct costs.

(d) The cost of having materials delivered ('carriage inwards') may be a direct cost if it is sufficiently large and can be associated with a particular product.

(e) The cost of materials wasted may be treated as a direct materials cost. This is considered in more detail below.

7.3 Indirect materials include items like consumable stores (such as rags or maintenance materials) and materials used in such small amounts that it is uneconomical to allocate them to a particular product, like the cost of glue in box-making.

Wastage

7.4 In a perfect world all materials issued to production would be used to make products, but in practice materials are often wasted. If you have ever started writing something on a piece of paper at work and then changed your mind and thrown that sheet in the bin then you have caused materials wastage.

7.5 Wastage can occur for a number of reasons.

(a) Due to human error: using the wrong grade or colour of material, cutting something inaccurately, drilling a hole in the wrong place and so on.

(b) Due to machine error: a machine may malfunction, damaging the materials it is currently working on in the process.

(c) Due to accident: for example, there may be a fire or a flood.

(d) Due to quality: if inferior quality materials are purchased they may not be suitable for the job. They may snap, bend, become discoloured and so on.

(e) Due to poor storage: materials may need to be kept dry, or protected from vermin.

(f) Due to age: some materials deteriorate with age. Foodstuffs are the most obvious examples, but other substances like paint may 'separate' and become unusable.

7.6 Another common reason for wastage is theft: do you ever write to a friend using a biro or stationery that you obtained from work? Petty pilfering is always a problem for businesses. If stocks are valuable and attractive there is also organised crime to contend with.

The cost of wastage

7.7 There are several ways in which wastage costs money.

(a) The materials wasted have been paid for, and usually have to be replaced.

(b) Production time may be lost through wastage since the product made may be worthless and unsaleable or extra time may be needed to rectify the fault.

(c) Disposing of wasted materials, such as cleaning up after a spill or paying somebody to take the material away, costs money.

7.8 In consolation, however, money can sometimes be recovered when defective materials are sold as scrap. This income can be netted off against the cost of the wastage.

Example: Wastage and scrap proceeds

7.9 Careless Ltd bought 5,000 kg of materials but due to a machine error 400 kg were damaged and had to be replaced. Materials cost £5 per kg and if damaged can be sold for £2 per kg. What is the materials cost of the job? What is the cost of the wastage?

Solution: Wastage and scrap proceeds

7.10

	£
Materials (5,000 × £5)	25,000

	£
Wastage (400 kg × £5)	2,000
Less sales proceeds (400kg × £2)	(800)
Cost of wastage	1,200

7.11 One question that should have occurred to you is whether the cost of wastage is a cost of production. The answer depends upon how the wastage occurred. If it is due to something that happened during the production process then it is a production cost. If not (for example if materials are stolen or damaged in storage) then it is not.

7.12 There are two ways of dealing with wastage that occurs during production. If it is a one-off loss it is charged as a direct cost of the particular job concerned (as in the example above). If, however, it is quite normal for there to be some wastage - wood off-cuts or fabric trimmings for example - the costs of the wastage are treated as production overheads. As we shall see later, this means that the costs are spread across all of the work done in a period, rather than attached to a specific job.

Key points in this chapter

- There are many different types of materials and a number of ways in which they may be classified.

- The materials cycle involves buying materials, storing them, using them and re-ordering them.

- There are several different ways of valuing materials used and materials remaining in stock: the main ones are FIFO, LIFO and weighted average cost.

- Materials costing requires a good understanding of stock control procedures and documentation.

- Computers are used extensively for stock control because they save a great deal of administrative effort.

- It is important to establish stock control levels to ensure the continuity of production and to minimise costs.

- Materials wastage costs money but sometimes money can be recovered when wasted materials are sold as scrap.

For practice on the points covered in this chapter you should now attempt the Exercises in Session 2 of the Cost Information Workbook

3 Labour costs

This chapter covers the following topics.

1   Determining labour costs

2   Recording labour costs

3   Overtime, bonuses and absences

4   Labour turnover

5   Direct and indirect labour costs

---

1 DETERMINING LABOUR COSTS

What are labour costs?

1.1 Labour costs could be said to include any or all of the following items.

(a) The gross amount due to the employee
(b) Employer's national insurance
(c) Amounts paid to recruit labour
(d) Amounts paid for staff welfare
(e) Training costs
(f) The costs of benefits like company cars

The list could be extended, but we shall not go any further because in this chapter we are only concerned with item (a), the employee's gross salary.

1.2 The word 'labour' is generally associated with strenuous physical effort but in the context of cost accounting it is not confined to manual work. Labour costs are the amounts paid to any employee, including supervisors, office staff, managers and tea ladies. We shall distinguish between direct labour and indirect labour, but even then you must not assume that this is necessarily a manual/clerical distinction. For example, most or all of the 'direct labour cost' of an audit is the result of its being done by highly paid and highly qualified pen-pushers (accountants)!

Labour costs and payroll

1.3 NVQ level 2 includes a unit on *Recording and accounting for payroll transactions* (Unit 3) and so you are not required for Unit 6 to deal with the nitty gritty of PAYE, National Insurance and so on. Obviously, however, there is a link between the methods of finding out the cost of labour and the systems for actually putting that amount in the pockets of employees, the government or anybody else who is entitled to a share.

1.4 One of the functions of payroll processing and accounting is to provide some of the basic data for analysing the costs of an enterprise and you will therefore see frequent references in the paragraphs that follow to payroll and to systems and documentation that you may previously have associated solely with payroll, and not with costing.

Determining labour costs

1.5 There are three ways in which labour costs can be determined.

(a) According to some prior agreement

(b) According to the amount of time worked

(c) According to the amount and/or quality of work done (piecework or performance based remuneration).

1.6 Payment for most jobs is by a combination of methods (a) and (b). There will be a 'basic' wage or salary which is agreed when the appointment is made. There will be a set number of hours per week during which the employee is expected to be available for work. There will be extra payments for time worked over and above the set hours, or deductions for time when the employee is not available beyond an agreed limit.

2 RECORDING LABOUR COSTS

2.1 You can see from the previous section that records of labour costs fall into three categories.

    (a)   Records of agreed basic wages and salaries
    (b)   Records of time spent
    (c)   Records of work done

2.2   There are a number of ways in which this can be organised, but basically the information flows will be as follows.

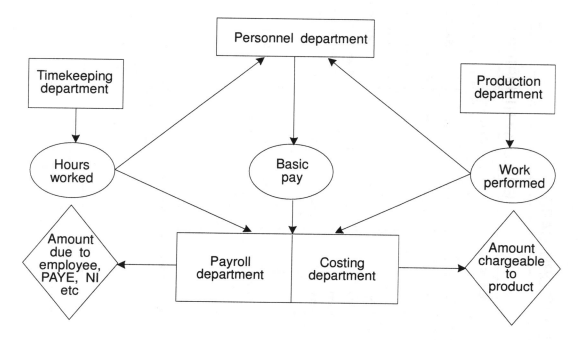

2.3   In practice timekeeping would probably be a sub-function of production or of personnel, or else personnel may keep records of hours on the premises and available for work, while the production department keeps records of time spent doing different tasks. The system used will depend upon the nature of the job and the bases chosen for paying employees on the one hand and for costing products on the other.

2.4   Information flows back to the personnel department so that employees can be considered for promotion or disciplined if appropriate.

2.5   All the information may, in practice, be given first to payroll, who would then pass it on for costing analysis, or vice versa. (Remember that in some organisations payroll administration is contracted out to a third party.) The main point is that both payroll and costing need the same information, but they analyse it differently: payroll asks 'who', and costing asks 'what'.

Basic pay

2.6   Levels of basic pay are ultimately decided by senior management who will take into account what other employers are paying for similar work, what they consider the work to be worth, how easy it is to recruit labour and any agreements with trade unions.

2.7   The basic pay due to an individual worker will be mentioned in his or her letter of appointment and included in his or her contract of employment. The main on-going record, however, will probably be kept on an employee record card held in the personnel department. This will also show subsequent increases in the wage rate or salary level and much other information. An example of an employee record card is shown on the following page.

2.8   Much of the information on the employee record card is confidential and there is no need for staff in the payroll department or the costing department to know about it.

PERSONNEL RECORD CARD

NUMBER   NAME   OTHER, A.N.

PERSONAL DETAILS

SURNAME   OTHER

FORENAMES   ALBERT NEIL

SEX (M) F	Nationality British
	Social Security Number WD 48 47 41C

Date of Birth   1 June 19X9

Marital Status   Single (Married) Separated Divorced Widowed

Dependants   None

Disabilities   None

Pension Scheme
Eligible   19X9 January
Joined   19X9 January

ADDRESS
94 Bootsale House
Antique Street
Old Salum
MERSEY ME5

Telephone   01973 89521

ADDRESS   1ST CHANGE
17 Newton Close
Brookeside
MERSEY ME1

Telephone   01973 12221

ADDRESS   2ND CHANGE

Telephone

Professional Qualifications
Accounting Technician 19X9

Educational Details

Higher Education

A levels   Economics (C)

BTec   Computer Services

GCSE   n/a

O levels   3

CSEs   4

Other   City & Guilds Photography

IN EMERGENCY CONTACT

Name   Other, Noreen Olga   Wife
Address
17 Newton Close
Brookeside
MERSEY ME1

Telephone (h)   01973 12221
Telephone (wk)   01973 51443

EMPLOYMENT HISTORY

Years of Service (12 months to 31 December)
1 2 3 4 5 6 7 8 9 10 11 12 13 14 15 16 17 18 19 20 21 22

FROM	TO	TITLE	DEPT	REASON	PAY
1/1/X8	31/3/X8	Junior Clerk	Sls Ledger	1st job here	£6,500
1/4/X8	30/6/X8			Probation period over	£7,000
1/7/X8				Annual payrise 5%	£7,350
1/X9		Senior Clerk	Pur Ledger	Got AAT Quals & promoted	£9,000
7/X9				10% pay rise	£9,900
7/Y0				10% (8% + 2% merit)	£10,890
12/Y0		Asst Technician	Payroll	Transfer	£10,890

Training History

Course Code	
0713/I	Induction to new employees

Special Details

Leave Entitlement   20 days

Ideally, therefore, details of basic pay for all employees are compiled on separate lists which are given to payroll and costing. A fresh list should be issued whenever the pay rates are revised.

2.9 In a computerised wage system, the basic rates are usually part of a database, and payroll and costing are only able to access information that is relevant to their tasks. Costing, for example, does not need to know the names of individual employees: in fact it is more efficient for workers to be coded according to the department they work in and the type of work that they do.

Standard costs

2.10 We shall discuss standard costs of labour later in this Tutorial Text, but we should mention here that if standard costing is in use then standard rates will be used to determine the labour cost of products. Actual data is still needed, however, to calculate variances.

Time records and performance records

Attendance time

2.11 The bare minimum record of employees' time is a simple attendance record showing days absent because of holiday, sickness or other reason. Such a system is usually used when it is assumed that all of the employees' time is taken up doing one job and no further analysis is required. A typical record of attendance is shown on the next page.

2.12 The next step up is to have some record of time of arrival, time of breaks and time of departure. The simplest form is a 'signing-in' book at the entrance to the building with, say, a page for each employee. Unless someone is watching constantly, however, this system is open to abuse and many employers use a time recording clock which stamps the time on a clock card inserted by the employee. A clock card is illustrated overleaf. More modern systems involve the use of a plastic card like a credit card which is 'swiped' through a device which makes a computer record of the time of arrival and departure.

2.13 The next step is to analyse the hours spent at work according to what was done during those hours. The method adopted depends upon the size of the organisation and the nature of the work.

Detailed analysis of time: continuous production

2.14 Where routine, repetitive work is carried out it might not be practical to record the precise details. For example if a worker stands at a conveyor belt for seven hours his work can be measured by keeping a note of the number of units that pass through his part of the process during that time. If a group of employees all contribute to the same process, the total units processed per day (or week or whatever) can be divided by the total number of hours they collectively worked.

No					Ending	
Name						

	HOURS	RATE	AMOUNT	DEDUCTIONS		
Basic				Income Tax		
O/T				NI		
Others				Other		
				Total deduction		
Total						
Less deductions						
Net due						

Time	Day		Basic time	Overtime
1230	T			
0803	T			
1700	M			
1305	M			
1234	M			
0750	M			

Signature --

NAME: A.N. OTHER **DEPT:** 072 **NI REF:** WD 4847 41C **LEAVE ENTITLEMENT:** 20

	1	2	3	4	5	6	7	8	9	10	11	12	13	14	15	16	17	18	19	20	21	22	23	24	25	26	27	28	29	30	31
JAN																															
FEB																															
MAR																															
APR																															
MAY																															
JUNE																															
JULY																															
AUG																															
SEPT																															
OCT																															
NOV																															
DEC																															

Illness : I
Industrial Accident : IA
Maternity : M

Leave : L
Unpaid Leave : UL
Special Leave : SL

Training : T
Jury Service : J

Note overleaf: (1) The reasons for special leave (eg bereavement).

(2) Ensure training is noted on personnel card.

RECORD OF ATTENDANCE

Example: Labour cost of continuous production

2.15 Team A comprises four members who are all paid £5 per hour and work a 35 hour week. During a particular week they processed 280 units. Calculate the following.

(a) The number of units Team A processes per hour
(b) The time is takes Team A to process one unit
(c) The labour cost of one unit

Solution: Labour cost of continuous production

2.16 (a) $\dfrac{\text{Total units processed}}{\text{Total man hours}} = \dfrac{280}{4 \times 35} = \dfrac{280}{140} = 2$ units per hour

(b) $\dfrac{\text{Total man hours}}{\text{Total units processed}} = \dfrac{4 \times 35}{280} = \dfrac{140}{280} = \frac{1}{2}$ hour per unit

(c) $\dfrac{\text{Total wages}}{\text{Total units processed}} = \dfrac{4 \times 35 \times £5}{280} = \dfrac{700}{280} = £2.50$ per unit

Detailed analysis of time: job costing
Centrally assessed 12/95

2.17 When the work is not of a repetitive nature the records required might be one or several of the following.

(a) *Daily time sheets*. These are filled in by the employee to indicate the time spent on each job. The total time on the time sheet should correspond with time shown on the attendance record. Times are recorded daily and so there is less risk that they will be forgotten but this system does produce considerable paperwork.

(b) *Weekly time sheets*. These are similar to daily time sheets but are passed to the cost office at the end of the week. Paperwork is reduced and weekly time sheets are particularly suitable where there are few job changes in a week.

(c) *Job cards*. Cards are prepared for each job (or operation forming part of a complete job) unlike time sheets which are made out for each employee. When an employee works on a job he or she records on the job card the time spent on that job. Job cards also carry instructions to the operator on how the job is to be carried out. Such records reduce the amount of writing to be done by the employee and therefore the possibility of error.

(d) *Route cards*. These are similar to job cards, except that they follow the product through the works and carry details of all operations to be carried out. They thus carry the cost of all operations involved in a job and are very useful for control purposes.

2.18 *Remember* that wages are calculated on the basis of the hours noted on the attendance card, whereas production costs are obtained from the time sheets/job cards/route cards.

2.19 The manual recording of times on time sheets or job cards is, however, liable to error or even deliberate deception, and may be unreliable. A time clock or automated time recording system is more accurate.

2.20 Time sheets and job or route cards can take many different forms, some of which involve computerised systems of time-recording. The following examples may help to indicate the basic principles of recording labour costs of production work.

Job No.	Start Time	Finish Time	Qty	Checker	Hrs	Rate	Extension

Time Sheet No. ....

Employee Name................. Clock Code................. Dept ....

Date........................... Week No. ....

JOB CARD

Department _ _ _ _ _ _ _ _ _ _ _ _ _ _ _ _ _ _.   Job no _

Date _ .   Operation no _ _ _ _ _ _ _ _ _ _ _ _ _ _ _ _ _

Time allowance _ _ _ _ _ _ _ _ _ _ _ _ _ _ _ _ _   Time started _ .

Time finished _ _ _ _ _ _ _ _ _ _ _ _ _ _ _ _ _ _ _

Hours on job   _ _ _ _ _ _ _ _ _ _ _ _ _ _ _ _ _ _ _ .

Description of job	Hours	Rate	Cost

Employee no _ _ _ _ _ _ _ _ _ _ _ _ _ _ _ _   Certified by _ _ _ _ _ _ _ _ _ _ _ _ _ _ _ _ _ _

Signature _

2.21   The time sheet will be filled in by the employee, for hours worked on each job (job code) or area of work (cost code). The cost of the hours worked will be entered at a later stage in the accounting department.

A job card will be given to the employee, showing the work to be done and the expected time it should take. The employee will record the time started and time finished for each job. Breaks for tea and lunch may be noted on the card, as standard times, by the production planning department. The hours actually taken and the cost of those hours will be calculated by the accounting department.

Salaried labour

2.22   You might think there is little point in salaried staff filling in a detailed timesheet about what they do every hour of the day, as their basic pay is a flat rate every month but, in fact, in many enterprises they are required to do so. There are a number of reasons for this.

(a)   Such timesheets aid the creation of management information about product costs, and hence profitability.

(b) The timesheet information may have a direct impact on the revenue the enterprise receives (see below).

(c) Timesheets are used to record hours spent and so support claims for overtime payments by salaried staff.

2.23 Below is shown the type of time sheet which can be found in large firms in the service sector of the economy: examples would be a firm of solicitors, a firm of accountants, or a firm of management consultants.

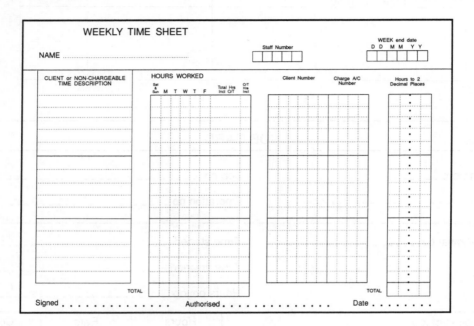

2.24 Service firms are chiefly in the business of selling the time and expertise of their employees to clients. This means that if an employee spends an hour at a particular client, the client will be billed for one hour of the employee's time. A time sheet is necessary so that clients will be charged for the correct amount of time that has been spent doing their work.

Idle time

2.25 In many jobs there are times when, through no fault of their own, employees cannot get on with their work. A machine may break down or there may simply be a temporary shortage of work.

2.26 Idle time has a cost because employees will still be paid their basic wage or salary for these unproductive hours and so there should be a record of idle time. This may simply comprise an entry on time sheets coded to 'idle time' generally, or separate idle time cards may be prepared. A supervisor might enter the time of a stoppage, its cause, its duration and the employees made idle on an idle time record card. Each stoppage should have a separate reference number which can be entered on time sheets or job cards as appropriate.

Measurement by output

2.27 The labour cost of work done by pieceworkers is determined from what is known as a piecework ticket or an operation card. The card records the total number of items (or 'pieces') produced and the number of rejects. Payment is only made for 'good' production.

```
┌─────────────────────────────────────────────────────────────────────┐
│                        OPERATION CARD                                 │
│                                                                       │
│   Operator's Name...................    Total Batch Quantity.......... │
│                                                                       │
│   Clock No..........................    Start Time ................... │
│                                                                       │
│   Pay week No........... Date .......    Stop Time .................... │
│                                                                       │
│   Part No...........................    Works Order No............... │
│                                                                       │
│   Operation.........................    Special Instructions ......... │
├──────────────────┬──────────────┬─────────────────┬──────────┬───────┤
│ Quantity Produced│  No Rejected │ Good Production │   Rate   │   £   │
│                  │              │                 │          │       │
│                  │              │                 │          │       │
│                  │              │                 │          │       │
│                  │              │                 │          │       │
│                  │              │                 │          │       │
├──────────────────┴──────────────┴─────────────────┴──────────┴───────┤
│   Inspector.........................    Operative .................... │
│                                                                       │
│   Foreman ..........................    Date ......................... │
├───────────────────────────────────────────────────────────────────────┤
│   PRODUCTION CANNOT BE CLAIMED WITHOUT A PROPERLY SIGNED CARD          │
└─────────────────────────────────────────────────────────────────────┘
```

Coding of job costs

2.28 By now you will appreciate that to analyse labour costs effectively it is necessary to be able to link up different pieces of information in various ways. Most organisations therefore develop a series of codes to facilitate analysis for each of the following.

(a) Employee number and perhaps a team number

(b) Pay rate, for example 'A' for £5 per hour, 'B' for £6 per hour and so on

(c) Department and/or location if the organisation has different branches or offices

(d) Job or batch type, for example different codes for audit, accounts preparation and tax in a firm of accountants, or for bodywork and mechanical repairs in a garage

(e) Job or batch number to enable each successive example of the same type of work to be allocated the next number in sequence

(f) Client number so that all work done for the same client or customer can be coded to the same number

2.29 You might like to think of different ways in which different pieces of information could be grouped together. For example, combining (b), (c) and (d) would show you whether the workers in one location could do a certain type of work more cheaply than the workers in another location.

3   OVERTIME, BONUSES AND ABSENCES

3.1 This section is concerned with two things: what happens when more or less work is done than the basic amount agreed and the consequences of not coming to work.

Overtime

3.2 If an employee works for more hours than the basic daily requirement many organisations pay an extra amount.

3.3   The overtime payment may simply be at the basic rate. If an employee earns £5 an hour he will get an extra £5 for every hour worked in addition to the basic hours. If he earns £10,000 a year an hourly rate can be calculated by multiplying the basic hours per day by the normal number of days worked per week by the 52 weeks in the year. For example 7 hours × 5 days × 52 weeks = 1,820 hours and the hourly rate is approximately £5.49.

3.4   Usually, however, overtime is paid at a premium rate. You will hear expressions like 'time and a third', ' time and a half' and so on. This means that the hourly rate for overtime hours is $(1 + \frac{1}{3})$ × basic rate or $(1 + \frac{1}{2})$ × basic rate.

Example: Overtime premium

3.5   Littletons Ltd pays overtime at time and a quarter. Lizzie's basic hours are 9 to 5 with an hour for lunch, but one particular Friday she worked until six o'clock. She is paid a basic wage of £5 per hour. How much did she earn on the Friday in question, and how much of this is overtime premium?

Solution: Overtime premium

3.6   The most obvious way of calculating the amount earned is as follows.

	£
Basic time (7 × £5)	35.00
Overtime ($1\frac{1}{4}$ × £5)	6.25
Total pay	41.25

3.7   It is wrong, however, to say that the overtime premium is £6.25. For costing purposes all of the hours worked, whether in basic time or outside it, are costed at the *basic rate*. The premium is the *extra* amount paid on top of the basic rate for the hours worked over and above the basic hours.

	£
Basic pay (8 × £5)	40.00
Overtime premium ($\frac{1}{4}$ × £5)	1.25
	41.25

3.8   The overtime premium is thus £1.25. This is an important point because overtime premium is usually treated as an indirect cost. This is quite reasonable if you think about it. If you and your colleague use identical calculators it is reasonable to suppose that they cost the same amount to produce. It might be that one was assembled at 10 o'clock in the morning and the other at 10 o'clock at night but this doesn't make the calculators different from each other. They should therefore have the same cost and so most organisations treat overtime premium as an overhead and do not allocate it to the products manufactured outside basic hours.

3.9   There are two exceptions to this rule.

   (a) If overtime is worked at the specific request of a customer to get his order completed, the premium is a direct cost of the order.

   (b) If overtime is worked regularly by a production department in the normal course of operations, the overtime paid to direct workers could be incorporated into an average direct labour hourly rate (though it does not need to be).

Incentives and bonuses

3.10   Overtime premiums are paid to encourage staff to work longer hours than normal (or at least to recognise and reward the personal sacrifice of doing so). Incentives and bonuses are paid to encourage staff to work harder whatever the time of day.

3.11 The range statement for the labour costs part of Unit 6 uses the expression *payment by results* for this type of remuneration. Another name used nowadays is *performance-related pay*. The paragraphs below describe examples of incentive schemes.

Piecework

3.12 Pieceworking can be seen as an incentive scheme: the more output you produce the more you are paid. If you are paid 5p per unit produced and you want to earn £300 gross a week you know you have to produce 6,000 units that week.

3.13 The system can be further refined by paying a different rate for different levels of production (differential piecework). For example the employer could pay 3p per unit for output of up to 3,500 a week, 5p per unit for every unit over 3,500.

3.14 In practice, persons working on such schemes normally receive a guaranteed minimum wage because they may not be able to work because of problems outside their control.

Time-saved bonus

Centrally assessed 6/97

3.15 Suppose that a garage has calculated that it takes an average of 45 minutes for an engineer to perform an MOT test, but the job could be done competently in 30 minutes. If the engineer is paid £6 per hour, the garage will save £1.50 on each MOT if the engineer only takes 30 minutes. The idea of a time-saved bonus is that some of this saving is paid to the engineer (maybe half).

3.16 There are problems with this approach. In the first place it is necessary to establish a standard time for all types of work, and this may not be easy. In the second place a less than competent engineer may rush the job and not do it properly.

Discretionary bonuses

3.17 It is not uncommon, especially in smaller businesses, for employers to give their employees bonuses simply because they think they deserve one. This is a possible approach if it is difficult to measure an employee's output. Many office workers fall into this category. If, however, there is no obvious correspondence between what a person does and whether or not a bonus is paid, the scheme is likely to be perceived as unfair.

Group bonus schemes

3.18 Sometimes it is not possible to measure individual effort because overall performance is not within any one person's control (for example railway workers). In such cases, however, it is possible to measure overall performance and a bonus can therefore be paid to all those who contributed.

Profit-sharing schemes

3.19 In a profit-sharing scheme employees receive a certain proportion of their company's year-end profits (the size of their bonus might also be related to level of responsibility and length of service).

Summary

3.20 The easier it is to measure output the more closely an incentive scheme can be tailored to individual performance. *In general*, in spite of the extra labour cost arising, the unit cost of output is reduced (because the labour time per unit is reduced) and so the profit earned per unit of sale is increased; in other words the profits arising from productivity improvements are shared between employer *and* employee. Bonus payments will generally be an indirect cost, since they cannot be directly linked with specific units of production.

Absence from work

3.21 An employee may be absent from work for a variety of reasons, the commonest being holidays, sickness, maternity and training.

3.22 The costs relating to absence through sickness, maternity and training are usually treated as an overhead rather than a direct cost of production. Although some organisations treat holiday pay as an overhead, the normal treatment is to regard it as a direct cost by charging an inflated hourly rate. Suppose an employee is normally paid £4 an hour for a 35 hour week and is entitled to four weeks annual holiday. He will therefore receive £560 (£4 × 35 × 4) holiday pay. Assuming that the employee works the remaining 48 weeks, his attendance time will total 1,680 (48 × 35) hours. Dividing £560 by 1,680 hours gives an addition of approximately 33p per hour to the employee's hourly rate to ensure that holiday pay is recovered.

3.23 Time absent because of holidays is paid at the normal basic rate, as is absence on training courses as a rule. There are statutory minimum levels for maternity pay and sickness pay, but above these employers can be as generous (or otherwise) as they wish.

4   LABOUR TURNOVER
Centrally assessed 12/96

4.1 People leave jobs for many different reasons. Sometimes the reasons for leaving have little to do with the jobs themselves. Staff may decide to move to a different area; older staff may retire.

4.2 Businesses are more likely to be concerned with departures that could have been prevented. As we shall see below, replacing staff can have a number of costs. Often also businesses lose the high quality staff they wish to retain, precisely because those people are of such quality that they find it easy to get jobs elsewhere.

Why do staff leave?

4.3 Low wages and benefits are often a significant reason. One consequence of the job insecurity of recent years is that many people have looked for other jobs and consequently there is a greater level of awareness of the market rates of pay for particular jobs. Additionally other benefits that are part of the remuneration package of a job will also be considered. These can include benefits such as company cars, subsidised canteens, health insurance and pension benefits.

4.4 Staff will also be concerned about their long term career prospects. Many will be more likely to leave if they believe that they have no chance of being promoted or otherwise advancing their career. They will also take account whether the business they work for demonstrates commitment to the long-term development of its staff by for example providing good training.

4.5 High staff turnover is also caused by poor working conditions. People may leave because they feel under too much stress or feel that the hours they are expected to work are too long. Physical factors such as inadequate air conditioning or poor natural light can be important.

4.6 The relationships between management and staff can be as important an influence as anything. Good management can lead to staff staying with a business because they feel loyal to their managers. By contrast poor management can have a devastating effect because it often affects all staff.

Replacement costs

4.7 If staff do leave and have to be replaced, a number of costs may result.

(a) Management may spend money advertising for new staff or paying the fees of recruitment agencies. Management time will also have to be spent interviewing people.

(b) There may be a gap between staff leaving and new staff joining, and hence a staff shortage which may mean output being lost.

(c) At least initially the productivity of new staff is likely to be lower than that of the staff they are replacing. New staff will also have to be trained, either on formal training courses or being given on the job training by other staff.

(d) Because new staff may lack experience of the work they are doing, there may be a greater risk of waste or production of substandard items, or a greater risk of tool or machine breakages.

Preventative costs

4.8 Management should however also be aware that if they want to prevent staff from leaving, there will be costs involved.

(a) It may be necessary to pay higher wages or provide a better benefits package.

(b) Training costs may increase but this increase should be matched by staff being better motivated and more productive.

5 DIRECT AND INDIRECT LABOUR COSTS
Centrally assessed 12/95 and 12/96

5.1 Generally direct labour costs will consist of the basic wages paid to staff who expend work on the product itself. Further guidelines which you may find useful are as follows.

(a) Overtime and bonus payments are generally an indirect cost as discussed above.

(b) Employer's national insurance contributions (which are added to employees' total pay as a wages cost) are frequently treated as an indirect labour cost. It is preferable, however, to calculate an inflated hourly rate as employer's national insurance contributions are a fundamental part of acquiring labour services.

(c) Idle time is an overhead cost, that is an indirect labour cost.

(d) The cost of work on capital equipment (see the next chapter) is incorporated into the capital cost of the equipment.

(e) Other indirect costs include training and the cost of the supervisor's wages.

Key points in this chapter

- Both costing and payroll use records of agreed basic wages or salaries, records of time spent and records of work done, but payroll asks 'who?' whereas costing asks 'what?'

- Time sheets, job cards and production records are the main sources of labour cost information.

- Overtime premiums, bonuses, incentive payments, payments during absence from work (except holiday pay) and payments when idle are all, as a rule, indirect labour costs.

- Staff turnover can give rise to a number of costs including recruitment and training costs, and the costs of lost output.

For practice on the points covered in this chapter you should now attempt the Exercises in Session 3 of the Cost Information Workbook

4 Expenses

This chapter covers the following topics.

1   Expense distinctions

2   Types of expenses

3   Depreciation and obsolescence

4   Recording and coding expenses

---

1   EXPENSE DISTINCTIONS

1.1   We have now looked in detail at materials costs and labour costs. In very simple terms 'expenses' are *any other* costs that might be incurred. We must, of course, make some finer distinctions than this.

Revenue and capital expenditure

Centrally assessed 12/95

1.2   *Capital expenditure* is expenditure which results in the acquisition of fixed assets or an improvement in their earning capacity. *Fixed assets* are assets which are acquired to provide benefits in more than one accounting period and are not intended to be resold in the normal course of trade.

(a)   Capital expenditure is not charged as an expense in the profit and loss account but a *depreciation charge* will usually be made to write capital expenditure off over time. Depreciation charges are expenses in the profit and loss account. For example, if an asset is bought for £20,000 and it is expected to last for 5 years, then for five years £4,000 per year will be charged to the profit and loss account.

(b)   Capital expenditure on fixed assets results in the appearance of a fixed asset in the balance sheet of the business.

1.3   *Revenue expenditure* is expenditure which is incurred for one of the following reasons.

(a)   For the purpose of the trade of the business, including expenditure classified as selling and distribution expenses, administration expenses and finance charges.

(b)   To *maintain* the *existing* earning capacity of fixed assets.

1.4   Revenue expenditure is charged to the profit and loss account in the period it is incurred, provided that it relates to the trading activity and sales of that particular period. For example, if a business buys 10 widgets for £200 (£20 each) and sells 8 of them during an accounting period, it will have 2 widgets left in stock at the end of the period. The full £200 is revenue expenditure but only £160 is a cost of goods sold during the period. The remaining £40 (cost of 2 widgets) will be included in the balance sheet in the stock of goods held as a current asset valued at £40.

Capital expenditure and revenue expenditure compared

1.5   Suppose that a business purchases a building for £30,000. It then adds an extension to the building at a cost of £10,000. The building needs to have a few broken windows mended, its floors polished and some missing roof tiles replaced. These cleaning and maintenance jobs cost £900.

1.6   In this example, the original purchase (£30,000) and the cost of the extension (£10,000) are capital expenditure because they are incurred to acquire and then improve a fixed asset. The other costs of £900 are revenue expenditure, because they merely maintain the building and thus the 'earning capacity' of the building.

1.7   The distinction between revenue items and capital items is that they are accounted for in different ways. The correct and consistent calculation of profit for any accounting period depends on the correct and consistent classification of items as revenue or capital.

Revenue and capital expenditure and costing

1.8   Revenue expenditure is much more relevant to the costing of products than capital expenditure, which is only of relevance when it is turned into revenue expenditure in the form of depreciation.

Direct and indirect expenses
Centrally assessed 12/95

1.9 A second major distinction that must be made is between direct and indirect expenses. You should know by now that a direct cost is a cost that can be traced in full to the product, service or department. An indirect cost (or overhead), on the other hand, is a cost that is incurred in the course of making a product, providing a service or running a department, but which is not traced directly or in full to the product, service or department.

1.10 Whereas most materials costs and (in a traditional manufacturing business) a large proportion of labour costs will be direct costs, most expenses are indirect costs. These will mostly not be related to production but be the costs of the other functions of a business, mainly distribution, selling, administration and finance.

1.11 Examples of direct expenses are:

(a) the cost of special designs, drawings or layouts

(b) the hire of tools or equipment for a particular job

(c) maintenance costs of tools and machines hired for a particular job

(d) power to run machines, *if* the machine is dedicated to producing a particular product

1.12 Examples of indirect expenses (overheads) are:

(a) factory rent (production overhead)

(b) power to run machines that are used to produce a large variety of products (production overhead)

(c) office insurance (administration overhead)

(d) market research (selling overhead)

(e) delivery vehicle petrol (distribution overhead)

Fixed and variable costs
Centrally assessed 12/95 and 6/97

1.13 We drew the distinction between fixed and variable costs in Chapter 1. Remember that *a fixed cost* is fixed no matter what the volume of activity is. A *variable cost* will vary according to the volume of activity.

1.14 Examples of fixed costs include rent for a building and building insurance. Examples of variable costs include direct material costs and charges for telephone calls. Certain variable costs may vary with the level of production, certain with the level of sales. For example commission paid on sales made will generally be a percentage of sales turnover.

1.15 In practice some costs are *semi-variable,* they will be incurred when output is nil, but also increase when output rises. Telephone expenses are an example; a business will have to pay a fixed rental charge even if no outward calls are made, but total charge will vary according to the volume of calls. You may also encounter *step costs* which are fixed only over a certain range. For example beyond a certain point stock will not fit in the warehouse, and extra storage space will therefore be required incurring extra costs.

1.16   Each of these costs can be represented graphically.

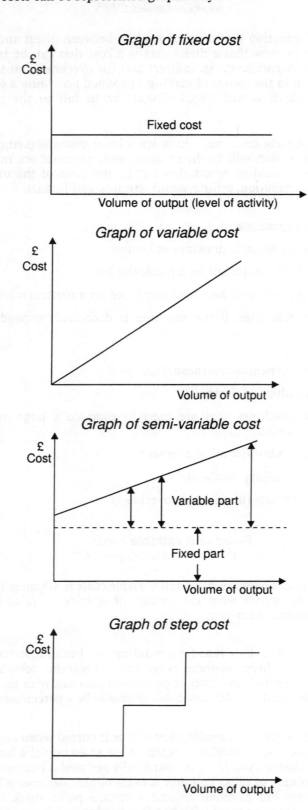

Graph of fixed cost

£
Cost

Fixed cost

Volume of output (level of activity)

Graph of variable cost

£
Cost

Volume of output

Graph of semi-variable cost

£
Cost

Variable part

Fixed part

Volume of output

Graph of step cost

£
Cost

Volume of output

Labour costs and expenses

1.17   The final distinction that should be made is between an organisation's own labour costs and the costs of services performed by people belonging to other organisations. Office cleaning is a good example. In whatever way this is paid for, the service you get involves a person going round the office with a hoover and a can of furniture polish. The classification of the cost of this service depends, however, upon whether or not the cleaner is on the payroll of the organisation using the cleaner's service.

(a) If your organisation *employs* the cleaner, the cost of the cleaner's time is an indirect *labour* cost and the cost of the materials used an indirect *materials* cost.

(b) If your organisation pays another organisation to do its cleaning the whole cost of the service is an indirect *expense*. That is, if you receive a third party *invoice* for cleaning, it is an expense.

2 TYPES OF EXPENSES
Centrally assessed 6/96

2.1 Revenue expenditure other than materials and labour costs can arise for a number of different reasons.

(a) *Buildings costs*. The main types are rent, business rates and buildings insurance.

(b) The *costs of making buildings habitable*. Gas and electricity bills and water rates, repairs and maintenance costs and cleaning costs.

(c) *People-related costs*. These include expenditure on health and safety, the cost of uniforms, and the cost of staff welfare provisions like tea and coffee, canteen costs and staff training.

(d) *Machine operating costs*. Machines need fuel or power and they need to be kept clean and properly maintained. Machines also need to be insured. A proportion of the capital cost of the machines becomes revenue expenditure in the form of depreciation. Some machines are hired.

(e) *Information processing costs*. Associated with information processing are the costs of telephone, postage, fax, computer disks and stationery, as well as subscriptions to information sources, like trade journals.

(f) *Finance costs*. If there is a bank loan there will be interest and bank charges to pay, and if equipment is leased there will be lease interest. Dividends paid to shareholders, however, are not a cost: they are an appropriation of some of the income earned in excess of all costs.

(g) *Selling and distribution costs*. Selling expenses include advertising, the salaries and commissions of salesmen, and the costs of providing consumer service and after sales service. The organisation's finished product also has to be stored and then delivered to customers. Distribution expenses would therefore include warehouse charges, upkeep and running of delivery vehicles and carriage outwards.

(h) *Costs of dealing with the outside world*. These include fees paid to professionals like external auditors, surveyors or solicitors and the costs of marketing (such as market research) would all be collected under this heading.

2.2 A typical detailed profit and loss account might, therefore, have the following headings.

	£	£
Sales		X
Less cost of sales:		
opening stock	X	
materials	X	
labour	X	
depreciation	X	
power and fuel	X	
	X	
Less closing stock	(X)	
Cost of sales		(X)
Gross profit		X
Less costs of administration, distribution and selling:		
wages and salaries	X	
rent and rates	X	
insurance	X	
heat and light	X	
depreciation of office equipment	X	
repairs and maintenance	X	
cleaning	X	
telecommunications	X	
printing, postage and stationery	X	
hire of computer equipment	X	
advertising	X	
warehouse charges	X	
carriage outwards	X	
audit and accountancy fees	X	
bank charges	X	
interest	X	
		(X)
Profit before tax		X

2.3 The following paragraphs describe some of these expenses in more detail.

Rent

2.4 Rent is usually an annual charge payable quarterly in advance.

Business rates

2.5 These are charges levied by local authorities on non-domestic properties in their area. They are based upon a rateable value multiplied by a uniform rate. They are usually payable in two instalments in April and October each year.

Insurance costs

2.6 These comprise 'premiums' paid annually to an insurance company to cover the risk, say, of damage to buildings or their contents by fire, flood, explosions, theft and so on. Buildings insurance is usually based on the cost of rebuilding the property with adjustments to take account of the property's particular location.

2.7 Other types of insurance include employer's liability insurance (against the risk of harming employees), and vehicle insurance.

Electricity, gas and telecommunications

2.8 Electricity, gas and telecommunications charges have two elements, a fixed amount called a standing charge, generally payable quarterly, and a variable amount based on consumption. There are a number of rates depending on the status of the user (domestic/commercial/industrial) and the time of day the power is consumed or the calls are made.

Hire charges

2.9 Hire charges are sometimes payable on a time basis. For example a cement mixer may be hired for, say, £10 a day. Sometimes an additional charge is made for usage. A photocopier, for example, might have a meter on it showing how many copies had been made. The meter would be read periodically by the hire company and the invoice would include a charge for the number of copies made in the period.

Discretionary costs

2.10 Discretionary costs are, as you might expect, costs that are incurred at somebody's discretion. Whereas an organisation has to pay a certain amount for, say, electricity simply so that the business can function, other costs are not crucial to the short-term continuance of operations. The main examples are research and development costs, staff training and advertising.

3 DEPRECIATION AND OBSOLESENCE

Depreciation
Centrally assessed 12/96

3.1 We mentioned depreciation at the beginning of this chapter and described it as a method of writing off capital expenditure. Depreciation methods are discussed in more detail as part of Unit 4 on capital expenditure, but you will probably find a brief overview useful.

3.2 There are two principal methods of depreciating an asset, the 'straight line' method and the reducing balance method.

   (a) The *straight line method* charges an equal amount of depreciation each period. It is calculated as $\dfrac{\text{Cost - residual value}}{\text{Number of years}}$.

   (b) The *reducing balance method* charges the largest amount of depreciation at the beginning of an asset's life. As the asset grows older the amount charged each period gets steadily smaller. The amount charged each year will be a fixed percentage of the c/f amount of the asset at the start of the year.

Example: Depreciation methods

3.3 Two assets are purchased for £8,000 each. One is depreciated over four years using the straight line method and the other is depreciated at the rate of 25% per annum on the reducing balance. What is the value of each asset after four years and how much per year is charged to the profit and loss account?

Solution: Depreciation methods

	Asset A		Asset B	
	Balance sheet	*Profit and loss account*	*Balance sheet*	*Profit and loss account*
	£	£	£	£
Capital cost	8,000		8,000	
Year 1 charge	(2,000)	2,000	(2,000)	2,000
c/f	6,000		6,000	
Year 2 charge	(2,000)	2,000	1,500	1,500
c/f	4,000		4,500	
Year 3 charge	(2,000)	2,000	(1,125)	1,125
c/f	2,000		3,375	
Year 4 charge	(2,000)	2,000	(844)	844
c/f	-		2,531	

3.5 The profit and loss account charge for asset A is calculated by splitting the £8,000 capital cost into four. For asset B it is calculated by taking 25% of the opening balance each year. In theory asset B could continue to be depreciated for evermore.

3.6 In order to decide which method is most appropriate we need to think a little more about why we are depreciating the asset at all.

The objectives of depreciation accounting

3.7 If an asset is purchased for £8,000 at the beginning of the year and sold for £6,000 at the end of the year then it is reasonable to conclude that the cost of owning the asset for a year is £2,000. This £2,000 is a real cost and it is in addition to the costs of *using* the asset, like fuel and repairs costs.

3.8 If the business had not owned the asset it would not have been able to make its product. It is therefore reasonable that the £2,000 cost should be charged as a cost of the product (although we won't say how to do this, for now).

3.9 One of the objectives of depreciation accounting is therefore to find some way of calculating this cost of ownership.

3.10 Consider, however, the use of a machine that is constructed to do a specific job for a specific firm. It may last 20 years and yet be of no use to anybody else at any time. It is, however, hardly fair to charge the whole cost of the machine to the first product that it makes, or even to the first year's production. Very probably the products it is making in year 19 will be just as well made as the products made in year 1.

3.11 Thus a second objective of depreciation accounting is to spread out the capital cost of the asset over as long a period as the asset is used.

3.12 The answer to the question 'which method is best?' therefore depends upon the asset in question, the way it is used, the length of time it is used, and the length of time it is useful in the light of changes in products, production methods and technology.

Depreciation in practice

3.13 In practice the method most often used is the straight line method because it is simple and gives a reasonable approximation (given that depreciation is an estimate).

3.14 Typical depreciation rates under the straight line method are as follows.

Freehold land	Not depreciated
Freehold buildings	2% per annum (50 years)
Leasehold buildings	Over the period of the lease
Plant and machinery	10% per annum (10 years)
Fixtures and fittings	10% per annum (10 years)
Motor vehicles	25% per annum (4 years)

Note that these are not rules: businesses can choose whatever method or rate they think is most appropriate. Motor vehicles, for example, are often depreciated using the reducing balance method since it is well known that in reality they lose the largest proportion of their value in their first few years.

3.15 Sometimes you may encounter depreciation methods that try to measure the fall in value/cost of use more accurately. A typical example is the machine-hour method illustrated below.

Example: The machine-hour method

3.16 A machine costs £100,000 and it is estimated that it will be sold as scrap for £5,000 at the end of its useful life. Experience has shown that such machines can run for approximately 10,000 hours before they wear out. What is the depreciation charge for the first year if the machine was used for 1,500 hours?

Solution: The machine-hour method

3.17 The rate is calculated as follows.

$$\frac{\text{Cost} - \text{residual value}}{\text{Useful life}}$$

$$\frac{£(100,000 - 5,000)}{10,000 \text{ hours}} = £9.50 \text{ per machine hour}$$

The depreciation charge for the first year is therefore

$$1,500 \times £9.50 = £14,250$$

This method is all very well if there are only a few such assets and careful records are kept of operating times but it would be quite an administrative burden if there were many such machines with different values, different lives and different usage.

Obsolescence

3.18 Obsolescence is the loss in value of an asset because it has been superseded, for example due to the development of a technically superior asset or changes in market conditions. As the loss in value is due to quite another reason than the 'wear and tear' associated with depreciation and because obsolescence may be rapid and difficult to forecast, it is not normal practice to make regular charges relating to obsolescence. Instead, the loss resulting from the obsolescence should be charged direct to the costing profit and loss account in the year obsolescence occurs.

4 RECORDING AND CODING EXPENSES
Centrally assessed 6/95 and 6/96

4.1 In this chapter we are only going to deal with the initial stages of recording expenses. Much more detail will be found in the following chapter which explains how overhead costs are attributed to the total costs of individual units of product.

Direct expenses

4.2   Direct expenses (such as plant hire for a specific job or solicitor's fees for drawing up a contract to provide a service) can simply be coded to the appropriate job or client when the bill arrives and recorded together with other direct costs.

Indirect expenses

4.3   Indirect expenses are initially *allocated* to the appropriate *cost centres*. We met cost centres briefly in Chapter 1 but in case you have forgotten a cost centre is *something* (location, function, activity or item of equipment, say) which incurs costs that can be attributed to units of production (cost units). That 'something' may be any of the following.

	Examples	
Cost centre type	*Production*	*Service*
Location	Factory A	Top floor
Function	Finishing department	Accounts department
Activity	Painting	Invoicing
Item of equipment	Spray-gun	Computer

4.4   The decision as to which cost centre is the appropriate one for an expense depends upon the type of expense. Some expenses will be solely related to production or to administration or to selling and distribution and can easily be allocated to the appropriate cost centre. Other costs, however, will be shared between these various functions and so such costs cannot be allocated directly to one particular cost centre. Cost centres therefore have to be established for the initial allocation of such shared expenses. Examples of the latter type of expense are numerous: rent, rates, heating and lighting, buildings maintenance and so on.

Example: Overhead allocation

4.5   As an example of the coding, analysis and recording of indirect expenses and other overheads at the initial stage, consider the following example.

The weekly costs of All Ltd include the following.

Wages of foreman of Department A	£1,000
Wages of foreman of Department B	£1,200
Indirect materials consumed in Department A	£400
Rent of premises shared by Departments A and B	£1,500

All Ltd's cost accounting system includes the following cost centres.

Code	
101	Department A
102	Department B
201	Rent

Your task is to show how the costs will be initially coded.

Solution: Overhead allocation

4.6

	£	*Code*
Wages of foreman of Department A	1,000	101
Wages of foreman of Department B	1,200	102
Indirect materials consumed in Department A	400	101
Rent of premises shared by Departments A and B	1,500	201

4.7   You may think that this is so obvious as not to be worth explaining. You will certainly not be surprised to be told that the next stage is to share the rent paid between the two departments. Why, you might ask, do we not split the cost of rent straightaway and not bother with cost centre 201?

4.8 To answer this question consider the following extract from the cost accounts of All Ltd, several months after the previous example. Cost centre 201 is no longer used because nobody could see the point of it.

	Cost centre 101	102
	£	£
Wages	1,172.36	1,415.00
Materials	73.92	169.75
Rent	638.25	1,086.75

You have just received a memo telling you that starting from this month (to which the above figures relate), Department A is to pay 25% of the total rent for the premises shared with Department B and Department B is to be split into 2 departments, with the new department (C) paying 37% of the remaining rent charge. The manager of Department B is standing over you asking you how much his department's new monthly rent charge will be.

4.9 The answer is £815.06. More importantly the first thing you have to do to calculate the answer is to *recreate* the total cost information that used to be allocated to cost centre 201. This is not very difficult in the present example, but imagine that there were 10 cost centres sharing premises and the cost information was recorded in a bulky ledger. Do you think it would have been easy to spot that the monthly rent had increased to £1,725?

Documentation

4.10 There are several ways in which this initial allocation could be documented. A common method is to put a stamp on the invoice itself with boxes to fill in, as appropriate.

%	A/C	£	P
25%	101	431	25
47.25%	102	815	06
27.75%	103	478	69
TOTAL	201	1725	00

Approved		Date	
Authorised		Date	
Posted		Date	

4.11 The dividing up of the total cost into portions ('apportionment') is described in more detail in the next chapter, but hopefully you now appreciate the importance of the initial step, allocation.

Apportionment and responsibility accounting

4.12 The last point raises another important question. It is unlikely that the managers of departments A, B and C have any control over the amount of rent that is paid for the building. They need to be made aware that their part of the building is not free but they are not responsible for the cost. The person responsible for controlling the amount of a cost such as this is more likely to be a separate manager, who looks after the interests of all of the company's buildings.

4.13 If cost centre 201 is maintained it can therefore be used to collect all the costs that are the responsibility of the premises manager. This approach is known as *responsibility accounting* and such cost centres can be called *responsibility centres*.

Cost codes
Centrally assessed 12/96

4.14 We have seen that charging costs to a cost centre involves two steps.

   (a) Identifying the cost centre for which an item of expenditure is a direct cost.
   (b) Allocating the cost to the cost centre.

4.15 The allocation of the cost to the cost centre is usually by means of a *cost code*.

4.16 In order to provide accurate management information, it is vital that costs are allocated correctly. Each individual cost should therefore be identifiable by its code. This is possible by building up the individual characteristics of the cost into the code.

4.17 The characteristics which are normally identified are as follows.

   (a) The nature of the cost (materials, labour, overhead) which is known as a *subjective classification*

   (b) The type of cost (direct or indirect and so on)

   (c) The cost centre to which the cost should be allocated. This is known as an *objective classification*.

   (d) The department which the particular cost centre is in.

Types of code

4.18 Some of the main coding methods are listed below.

   (a) *Sequence (or progressive) codes*

   Numbers are given to items in ordinary numerical sequence, so that there is no obvious connection between an item and its code. For example:

000042	2" nails
000043	office stapler
000044	hand wrench

   (b) *Group classification codes*

   These are an improvement on simple sequence codes, in that a digit (often the first one) indicates the classification of an item. For example:

4NNNNN	nails
5NNNNN	screws
6NNNNN	bolts

   (*Note.* 'N' stands for another digit; 'NNNNN' indicates there are five further digits in the code.)

   (c) *Faceted codes*

   These are a refinement of group classification codes, in that each digit of the code gives information about an item. For example:

(i) The first digit:

    1 Nails
    2 Screws
    3 Bolts
    etc...

(ii) The second digit:

    1 Steel
    2 Brass
    3 Copper
    etc...

(iii) The third digit:

    1 50 mm
    2 60 mm
    3 75 mm
    etc...

A 60mm steel screw would have a code of 212.

(d) *Significant digit codes*

These incorporate some digit(s) which is (are) part of the description of the item being coded. For example:

5000	screws
5050	50 mm screws
5060	60 mm screws
5075	75 mm screws

(e) *Hierarchical codes*

This is a type of faceted code where each digit represents a classification, and each digit further to the right represents a smaller subset than those to the left. For example:

3	=	Screws
31	=	Flat headed screws
32	=	Round headed screws
322	=	Steel (round headed) screws

and so on.

4.19 A coding system does not have to be structured entirely on any one of the above systems - it can mix the various features according to the items which need to be coded. But the system eventually chosen should always be simple to use and understand and it should be flexible (so that it can readily accommodate changes within an organisation, especially expansion).

The advantages of a coding system

4.20 (a) A code is usually briefer than a description, thereby saving clerical time in a manual system and storage space in a computerised system.

(b) A code is more precise than a description and therefore reduces ambiguity.

(c) Coding facilities data processing.

4.21 In Chapter 6 we show how a coding system which includes expense accounts and balance sheet accounts might be structured.

Key points in this chapter

- Expenses are costs other than materials or labour costs. They may be revenue or capital expenses. They may be direct or indirect. They may be fixed or variable.

- Revenue expenditure takes a wide variety of forms. One categorisation is buildings costs, people-related costs, machine-related costs, information processing costs, finance costs, selling and distribution costs and the costs of dealing with third parties.

- Depreciation is an expense. The aims of depreciation accounting are to calculate the cost of ownership and to spread the capital cost of an asset over the period for which the asset is used.

- Direct expenses are allocated directly to the product or service on behalf of which they are incurred.

- Indirect expenses are initially allocated to a single cost centre and then spread out over other cost centres that benefit from the expense.

For practice on the points covered in this chapter you should now attempt the Exercises in Session 4 of the Cost Information Workbook

5 Absorption costing

This chapter covers the following topics.

1   **What are overheads?**

2   **What is absorption costing?**

3   **Overhead apportionment**

4   **Overhead absorption**

5   **Separate departmental absorption rates**

6   **Over- and under-absorption**

7   **Predetermined rates and actual costs**

8   **Fixed and variable overheads and capacity**

9   **Activity based costing**

---

1 WHAT ARE OVERHEADS?
Centrally assessed 6/95

1.1 'What a stupid question' you may be thinking to yourself but you would be surprised by the number of students who are not 100% certain about overheads and what they are.

1.2 Overheads are actually the total of the following.

(a) Indirect materials
(b) Indirect labour
(c) Indirect expenses

(Note that in the previous chapter we were looking at *expenses*, whether they were direct or indirect.)

1.3 Before we go any further let us look at one common way of categorising overheads.

(a) Production overhead
(b) Production service overhead
(c) Administration overhead
(d) Selling and distribution overhead

These are similar to the categories described in Chapter 4.

1.4 There are a number of schools of thought as to the correct method of dealing with overheads.

(a) Absorption costing
(b) Activity based costing
(c) Marginal costing

We will be looking at absorption costing in detail in this chapter. Activity based costing will be covered more briefly. Marginal costing is not assessable at this level.

2 WHAT IS ABSORPTION COSTING?

2.1 The objective of absorption costing is to include in the total cost of a product (unit or job, say) an appropriate share of the organisation's total overhead. By an appropriate share we mean an amount that reflects the amount of time and effort that has gone into producing a unit or completing a job.

2.2 If an organisation had but one production department and produced identical units then the total overheads would be divided among the total units produced. Life is, of course, never that simple. Absorption costing is a method for sharing overheads between a number of different products on a fair basis.

The effect of absorption costing

2.3 Before describing the procedures by which overhead costs are shared out among products, it may be useful to consider the reasons why absorption costing is commonly used.

2.4 Suppose that a company makes and sells 100 units of a product each week. The direct cost per unit is £6 and the unit sales price is £10. Production overhead costs £200 per week and administration, selling and distribution overhead costs £150 per week. The weekly profit could be calculated as follows.

	£	£
Sales (100 units × £10)		1,000
Direct costs (100 × £6)	600	
Production overheads	200	
Administration, selling, distribution costs	150	
		950
Profit		50

2.5 In absorption costing, overhead costs will be added to each unit of product manufactured and sold.

	£ per unit
Direct cost per unit	6
Production overhead (£200 per week for 100 units)	2
Full factory cost	8

The weekly profit would be calculated as follows.

	£
Sales	1,000
Less factory cost of sales	800
Gross profit	200
Less administration, selling, distribution costs	150
Net profit	50

2.6 It may already be apparent that the weekly profit is £50 no matter how the figures have been presented. This being so, how does absorption costing serve any useful purpose in accounting? Is it necessary?

Is absorption costing necessary?
Centrally assessed 6/96

2.7 The reasons for using absorption costing have traditionally been identified as follows.

(a) *Stock valuations*. Stock in hand must be valued for two reasons.

(i) For the closing stock figure in the balance sheet

(ii) For the cost of sales figure in the profit and loss account. The valuation of stocks will actually affect profitability during a period because of the way in which cost of sales is calculated.

The cost of goods produced
+ the value of opening stocks
− the value of closing stocks
= the cost of goods sold.

In our example above, closing stocks could be valued at direct cost (£6), but in absorption costing, they would be valued at a fully absorbed factory cost of £8 per unit.

(b) *Pricing decisions*. Many companies attempt to fix selling prices by calculating the full cost of production or sales of each product, and then adding a margin for profit. In our example, the company might have fixed a gross profit margin at 25% on factory cost, or 20% of the sales price, in order to establish the unit sales price of £10. 'Full cost plus pricing' can be particularly useful for companies which do jobbing or contract work, where each job or contract is different, so that a standard unit sales price cannot be fixed. Without using absorption costing, a full cost is difficult to ascertain.

(c) *Establishing the profitability of different products*. This argument in favour of absorption costing is more contentious, but is worthy of mention here. If a company sells more than one product, it will be difficult to judge how profitable each individual product is, unless overhead costs are shared on a fair basis and charged to the cost of sales of each product.

Statement of standard accounting practice 9 (SSAP 9)

2.8 Of these three arguments, the problem of valuing stocks is perhaps the most significant, because absorption costing is recommended in financial accounting by the statement of standard accounting practice on stocks and long-term contracts (SSAP 9). SSAP 9 deals with financial accounting systems and not with cost accounting systems. The cost accountant is (in theory) free to value stocks by whatever method seems best, but where companies integrate their financial accounting and cost accounting systems into a single system of accounting records, the valuation of closing stocks will be determined by SSAP 9.

Costing procedures

2.9 The three stages of calculating the costs of overheads to be charged to manufactured output are allocation, apportionment and absorption. (Absorption costing is the name used since absorption is the ultimate aim of the other two procedures.)

(a) *Allocation* is the process which we met in the previous chapter. It is the assignment of costs to cost centres.

(b) *Apportionment* is the process by which cost items, or cost centre costs, are divided between several other cost centres in a 'fair' proportion. The reasons for needing apportionment are described later. We also encountered this briefly in the previous chapter and it is described in Section 3 of this chapter.

(c) *Absorption* is the process whereby costs of cost centres are added to unit, job or process costs. Overhead absorption is sometimes called 'overhead recovery'. It is described in Section 4 of this chapter.

3 OVERHEAD APPORTIONMENT
Centrally assessed 6/95, 12/95, 12/96 and 6/97

Stage one: sharing out common costs

3.1 Overhead apportionment follows on from overhead allocation. The first stage of overhead apportionment is to identify all overhead costs as production cost centre overhead, production service cost centre overhead, administration overhead or selling and distribution overhead. This means that the shared costs (such as rent and rates, heat and light and so on) initially allocated to a single cost centre for reasons explained in the previous chapter must now be shared out between the other (functional) cost centres.

Bases of apportionment

3.2 It is important that overhead costs are shared out on a fair basis but this is much more easily said than done. It is rarely possible to use only one method of apportioning costs to the various cost centres of an organisation. The bases of apportionment for the most usual cases are given below.

Overhead to which the basis applies	*Basis*
Rent, rates, heating and light, repairs and depreciation of buildings	Floor area occupied by each cost centre
Depreciation, insurance of equipment	Cost or book value of equipment
Personnel office, canteen, welfare, wages and cost offices, first aid	Number of employees, or labour hours worked in each cost centre
Heating, lighting (see above)	Volume of space occupied by each cost centre
Carriage inwards (costs paid for the delivery of material supplies)	Value of material issues to each cost centre

3.3 Don't forget that some overhead costs can be allocated to the user cost centre without having to be apportioned, for example indirect wages and consumable supplies.

Example: Overhead apportionment

3.4 Portion Ltd incurred the following overhead costs.

	£
Depreciation of factory	1,000
Factory repairs and maintenance	600
Factory office costs (treat as production overhead)	1,500
Depreciation of equipment	800
Insurance of equipment	200
Heating	390
Lighting	100
Canteen	900
	5,490

Information relating to the production and service departments in the factory is as follows.

	Department			
	Production A	Production B	Service X	Service Y
Floor space (sq. metres)	1,200	1,600	800	400
Volume (cubic metres)	3,000	6,000	2,400	1,600
Number of employees	30	30	15	15
Book value of equipment	£30,000	£20,000	£10,000	£20,000

How should the overhead costs be apportioned between the four departments?

Solution: Overhead apportionment

3.5

Item of cost	Basis of apportionment	Total cost	To Department			
			A	B	X	Y
		£	£	£	£	£
Factory depreciation	(floor area)	1,000	300	400	200	100
Factory repairs	(floor area)	600	180	240	120	60
Factory office	(no. of employees)	1,500	500	500	250	250
Equipment depn	(book value)	800	300	200	100	200
Equipment insurance	(book value)	200	75	50	25	50
Heating	(volume)	390	90	180	72	48
Lighting	(floor area)	100	30	40	20	10
Canteen	(no. of employees)	900	300	300	150	150
Total		5,490	1,775	1,910	937	868

Example: More overhead apportionment

3.6 Igg Ltd is preparing its production overhead budgets and determining the apportionment of those overheads to products. Cost centre expenses and related information have been budgeted as follows.

	Total £	Machine shop A £	Machine shop B £	Assembly £	Canteen £	Maintenance £
Indirect wages	78,560	8,586	9,190	15,674	29,650	15,460
Consumable materials (inc. maintenance)	16,900	6,400	8,700	1,200	600	-
Rent and rates	16,700					
Buildings insurance	2,400					
Power	8,600					
Heat and light	3,400					
Depreciation of machinery	40,200					
Value of machinery	402,000	201,000	179,000	22,000	-	-

Other information:

	Total	Machine shop A	Machine shop B	Assembly	Canteen	Maintenance
Power usage - technical estimates (%)	100	55	40	3	-	2
Direct labour (hours)	35,000	8,000	6,200	20,800	-	-
Machine usage (hours)	25,200	7,200	18,000	-	-	-
Area (sq ft)	45,000	10,000	12,000	15,000	6,000	2,000

How should the overheads be apportioned to the five cost centres?

Solution: More overhead apportionment

3.7

	Total £	A £	B £	Assembly £	Canteen £	Maintenance £	Basis of apportionment £
Indirect wages	78,560	8,586	9,190	15,674	29,650	15,460	Actual
Consumable materials	16,900	6,400	8,700	1,200	600	-	Actual
Rent and rates	16,700	3,711	4,453	5,567	2,227	742	Area
Insurance	2,400	533	640	800	320	107	Area
Power	8,600	4,730	3,440	258	-	172	Usage
Heat and light	3,400	756	907	1,133	453	151	Area
Depreciation	40,200	20,100	17,900	2,200	-	-	Value
	166,760	44,816	45,230	26,832	33,250	16,632	

Stage two: apportioning service cost centre costs to production cost centres

3.8 The second stage of overhead apportionment concerns the treatment of service cost centres. A factory is divided into several production cost centres and also many service cost centres, but only the production cost centres are directly involved in the manufacture of the units. In order to be able to add production overheads to unit costs, it is necessary to have all the overheads charged to (or located in) the production cost centres. The next stage in absorption costing is therefore to apportion the costs of service cost centres to the production cost centres.

3.9 There are two methods by which the apportionment of service cost centre costs can be done.

(a) Apportion the costs of each service cost centre to production cost centres only.

(b) Apportion the costs of each service cost centre not only to production cost centres, but also to other service cost centres which make use of its services, and eventually apportion all costs to the production cost centres alone by a gradual process of 'repeated distribution'.

3.10 Whichever method is used, the basis of apportionment must be fair and a different apportionment basis may be applied for each service cost centre. For example:

Service cost centre	Possible basis of apportionment
Stores	Number or cost value of material requisitions
Maintenance	Hours of maintenance and repair work done for each cost centre
Production planning	Direct labour hours worked for each production cost centre

Example: Direct apportionment

3.11 Reapportion Ltd incurred the following overhead costs.

	Production departments		Stores department	Maintenance department
	P	Q		
	£	£	£	£
Allocated costs	6,000	4,000	1,000	2,000
Apportioned costs	2,000	1,000	1,000	500
	8,000	5,000	2,000	2,500

Production department P requisitioned materials to the value of £12,000. Department Q requisitioned £8,000 of materials. The maintenance department provided 500 hours of work for department P and 750 for department Q. What are the total production overhead costs of Departments P and Q?

Solution: Direct apportionment

3.12

Service department	Basis of apportionment	Total cost	Dept P	Dept Q
		£	£	£
Stores	Value of requisitions	2,000	1,200	800
Maintenance	Direct labour hours	2,500	1,000	1,500
		4,500	2,200	2,300
Previously allocated and apportioned costs		13,000	8,000	5,000
Total overhead		17,500	10,200	7,300

Example: Direct apportionment again

3.13 Look back to the example solution in Paragraph 3.7. Using the bases of apportionment which you consider most appropriate from the information provided in Paragraph 3.6, calculate overhead totals for Igg Ltd's three production departments.

Solution: Direct apportionment again

3.14

	Total	A	B	Assembly	Canteen	Mainten-ance	Basis of appor-tionment
	£	£	£	£	£	£	£
Total overheads	166,760	44,816	45,230	26,832	33,250	16,632	
Reallocate	-	7,600	5,890	19,760	(33,250)	-	Dir labour
	-	4,752	11,880	-	-	(16,632)	Mac usage
Totals	166,760	57,168	63,000	46,592	-	-	

The repeated distribution method

3.15 Apportionment is a procedure whereby indirect costs are spread fairly between cost centres. It could therefore be argued that a fair sharing of service cost centre costs is not possible unless consideration is given to the work done by each service cost centre for other service cost centres.

3.16 For example, suppose a company has two production and two service departments (stores and maintenance). The following information about activity in the recent costing period is available.

	Production departments		Stores	Maintenance
	1	*2*	*department*	*department*
Overhead costs	£10,030	£8,970	£10,000	£8,000
Cost of material requisitions	£30,000	£50,000	-	£20,000
Maintenance hours needed	8,000	1,000	1,000	

The problem is that the stores department uses the maintenance department, and the maintenance department uses the stores.

(a) If service department overheads were apportioned directly to production departments, the apportionment would be as follows.

Service department	Basis of apportionment	Total cost	*1*	*2*
		£	£	£
Stores	(Material requisitions)	10,000	3,750	6,250
Maintenance	(Maintenance hours)	8,000	7,111	889
		18,000	10,861	7,139
Overheads of Department 1 and 2		19,000	10,030	8,970
		37,000	20,891	16,109

(b) If, however, recognition is made of the fact that the stores and maintenance department do work for each other, and the basis of apportionment remains the same, we ought to apportion service department costs as follows.

	Dept 1	Dept 2	Stores	Maintenance
Stores (100%)	30%	50%	-	20%
Maintenance (100%)	80%	10%	10%	-

This may be done using the repeated distribution method of apportionment, which is perhaps best explained by means of an example.

3.17

	Production dept 1	Production dept 2	Stores	Maintenance
	£	£	£	£
Overhead costs	10,030	8,970	10,000	8,000
Apportion stores (see note (a))	3,000	5,000	(10,000)	2,000
			0	10,000
Apportion maintenance	8,000	1,000	1,000	(10,000)
			1,000	0
Repeat: Apportion stores	300	500	(1,000)	200
Repeat: Apportion maintenance	160	20	20	(200)
Repeat: Apportion stores	6	10	(20)	4
Repeat: Apportion maintenance	4	-	-	(4)
	21,500	15,500	0	0

Notes

(a) The first apportionment could have been the costs of maintenance, rather than stores; there is no difference to the final results.

(b) When the repeated distributions bring service department costs down to small numbers (here £4), the final apportionment to production departments is an approximate rounding.

3.18 You should note the difference in the final overhead apportionments to each production department using the different apportionment methods. Unless the difference is substantial, the first method might be preferred because it is clerically simpler to use.

The algebraic method of apportionment

3.19 You may prefer this method to the repeated distribution method, especially if you are mathematically-minded, but it gives the same answer.

3.20 The total overhead costs of the various departments in the example above could be expressed as follows.

Dept 1:	£10,030 + 0.3s + 0.8m = x
Dept 2:	£8,970 + 0.5s + 0.1m = y
Stores:	£10,000 + 0.1m = s
Maintenance:	£8,000 + 0.2s = m

s and m in this equation stand for the total overhead costs of stores and maintenance respectively.

3.21 Hopefully you recognise the last two equations as very simple simultaneous equations which can be solved by substitution. For example we can substitute for m in the equation for s.

$$
\begin{aligned}
s &= 10,000 + 0.1 \times (8,000 + 0.2s) \\
&= 10,000 + 800 + 0.02s \\
0.98s &= 10,800 \\
s &= 11,020
\end{aligned}
$$

3.22 Now that we know the value of s we can find the value of m.

$$
\begin{aligned}
m &= 8,000 + 0.2s \\
&= 8,000 + 0.2 \times 11,020 \\
&= 10,204
\end{aligned}
$$

3.23 Now we can find the values of x and y

$$
\begin{aligned}
x &= 10,030 + (0.3 \times 11,020) + (0.8 \times 10,204) \\
&= 21,499 \\
y &= 8,970 + (0.5 \times 11,020) + (0.1 \times 10,204) \\
&= 15,500
\end{aligned}
$$

3.24 Allowing for rounding these are the same answers as we obtained in Paragraph 3.17.

4 OVERHEAD ABSORPTION
Centrally assessed 6/95 – 6/97

4.1 Having allocated and/or apportioned all overheads, the next stage in the costing treatment of overheads is to add them to, or absorb them into, cost units. We met *cost units* alongside cost centres in Chapter 1, but a reminder now will probably be helpful. The cost unit of a business is the thing that it sells. For the biro manufacturer it is the biro, or a box of 100 biros if he only sells them in that quantity. For a solicitor it is an hour of his time and there are as many more examples as there are different types of business.

Overheads are usually added to cost units using a *predetermined overhead absorption rate*, which is calculated using figures from the budget.

4.2 An overhead absorption rate for the forthcoming accounting period is calculated as follows.

(a) An estimate is made of the overhead likely to be incurred during the coming period.

(b) An estimate is made of the total hours, units, or direct costs or whatever it is upon which the overhead absorption rates are to be based (the *activity level*).

(c)   The estimated overhead is divided by the budgeted activity level. This produces the overhead absorption rate.

4.3   The overhead then 'gets into' the cost unit by *applying* the rate that has been calculated to the information already established for the cost unit. If overhead is absorbed at, say £2 per labour hour, then a cost unit that takes 3 labour hours to produce absorbs $3 \times £2 = £6$ in overheads. Let's look at a very simple example. It might help to make things clearer.

Example: The basics of absorption costing

4.4   Suppose total overhead is estimated to be £50,000 and total labour hours are expected to be 100,000 hours. The business makes two products, the abba and the zorba. Abbas take 2 labour hours each to make and zorbas take 5. What is the overhead cost per unit for abbas and zorbas respectively if overheads are absorbed on the basis of labour hours?

Solution: The basics of absorption costing

4.5   First calculate the absorption rate.

$$\text{Absorption rate} = \frac{\text{Total estimated overhead}}{\text{Total estimated activity level}} = \frac{£50,000}{100,000 \text{ hrs}}$$

$$= £0.50 \text{ per labour hour}$$

4.6   Now apply it to the products.

	Abba	*Zorba*
Labour hours per unit	2	5
Absorption rate per labour hour	£0.50	£0.50
Overhead absorbed per unit	£1	£2.50

Possible bases of absorption

4.7   The different bases of absorption (or 'overhead recovery rates') which can be used are as follows.

(a)   A percentage of direct materials cost
(b)   A percentage of direct labour cost
(c)   A percentage of total direct cost (prime cost)
(d)   A rate per machine hour
(e)   A rate per direct labour hour
(f)   A rate per unit
(g)   A percentage of factory cost (for administration overhead)
(h)   A percentage of sales or factory cost (for selling and distribution overhead)

4.8   Which basis should be used for production overhead depends largely on the organisation concerned. As with apportionment it is a matter of being fair.

4.9   Percentages of materials cost, wages or direct cost should be adopted only where the value of the materials and/or wages is considered to have some relationship with the overhead. For example, it is safe to assume that the indirect costs for producing brass screws are similar to the indirect costs for producing steel screws, but the cost of brass is very much greater than that of steel. Consequently, the overhead charge for brass screws would be too high and that for steel screws too low, if a percentage of cost of materials rate were to be used. A similar argument applies if a wages based rate is used: a unit produced by a trained mechanic would be charged with too much overhead whereas one produced by an apprentice would be charged with too little.

4.10 Note in particular that a rate per unit is only effective if all units are identical and therefore give rise to an identical amount of overhead.

4.11 Many factories therefore use the direct labour hour rate or machine hour rate in preference to a rate based on a percentage of direct materials cost, wages or prime cost. A machine hour rate would be used in departments where production is controlled or dictated by machines. In such a situation, where a small number of workers supervise a process that is performed almost entirely by machine, the distinction between direct and indirect labour may be difficult to identify, and labour costs may not be the principal costs of production. A direct labour hour basis is more appropriate in a labour intensive environment. We shall return to this point at the end of this chapter.

Example: Overhead absorption rates

4.12 The budgeted production overheads and other budget data of Clive Ltd are as follows.

Budget	*Production dept A*	*Production dept B*
Overhead cost	£36,000	£5,000
Direct materials cost	£32,000	
Direct labour cost	£40,000	
Machine hours	10,000	
Direct labour hours	18,000	
Units of production		1,000

What would the absorption rate be for each department using the various bases of apportionment?

Solution: Overhead absorption rates

4.13 (a) Department A

   (i) % of direct materials cost $\dfrac{£36,000}{£32,000} \times 100\% = 112.5\%$

   (ii) % of direct labour cost $\dfrac{£36,000}{£40,000} \times 100\% = 90\%$

   (iii) % of total direct cost $\dfrac{£36,000}{£72,000} \times 100\% = 50\%$

   (iv) Rate per machine hour $\dfrac{£36,000}{10,000 \text{ hrs}} = £3.60$ per machine hour

   (v) Rate per direct labour hour $\dfrac{£36,000}{18,000 \text{ hrs}} = £2$ per direct labour hour

   (b) For department B the absorption rate will be based on units of output.

   $\dfrac{£5,000}{1,000 \text{ units}} = £5$ per unit produced

Example: Overhead absorption rates once more

4.14 Using the information in Paragraph 3.6 and the example solution in Paragraph 3.14, determine budgeted overhead absorption rates for each of Igg Ltd's production departments using bases of absorption which you consider most appropriate from the information provided.

Solution: Overhead absorption rates once more

4.15 Machine shop A: $\dfrac{£57,168}{7,200} = £7.94$ per machine hour

Machine shop B: $\dfrac{£63,000}{18,000} = £3.50$ per machine hour

Assembly: $\dfrac{£46,592}{20,800} = £2.24$ per direct labour hour

The effect on total cost of applying different bases

4.16 The choice of the basis of absorption is significant in determining the cost of individual units, or jobs, produced. Using the example in Paragraphs 4.12 and 4.13, suppose that in department A an individual product has a materials cost of £80, a labour cost of £85, and requires 36 labour hours and 23 machine hours to complete. The overhead cost of the product would vary, depending on the basis of absorption used by the company for overhead recovery.

(a) As a percentage of direct material cost, the overhead cost would be

$$112.5\% \times £80 = £90.00$$

(b) As a percentage of direct labour cost, the overhead cost would be

$$90\% \times £85 = £76.50$$

(c) As a percentage of total direct cost, the overhead cost would be

$$50\% \times £165 = £82.50$$

(d) Using a machine hour basis of absorption, the overhead cost would be

$$23 \text{ hrs} \times £3.60 = £82.80$$

(e) Using a labour hour basis, the overhead cost would be $36 \text{ hrs} \times £2 = £72.00$

4.17 In theory, each basis of absorption would be possible, but the company should choose a basis for its own costs which seems to be 'fairest'. In our example, this choice will be significant in determining the cost of individual products, as the following summary shows. However the total cost of production overheads is the estimated overhead expenditure, no matter what basis of absorption is selected. It is the relative share of overhead costs borne by individual products and jobs which is affected by the choice of overhead absorption basis.

4.18 A summary of the product costs for the example beginning in Paragraph 4.12 is shown below.

| | Basis of overhead recovery | | | | |
| | *Percentage of materials cost* | *Percentage of labour cost* | *Percentage of prime cost* | *Machine hours* | *Direct labour hours* |
	£	£	£	£	£
Direct material	80	80.0	80.0	80.0	80
Direct labour	85	85.0	85.0	85.0	85
Production overhead	90	76.5	82.5	82.8	72
Full factory cost	255	241.5	247.5	247.8	237

The arbitrary nature of absorption costing

4.19 Absorption costing may irritate you because, even if a company is trying to be 'fair', there is a great lack of precision about the way an absorption base is chosen.

4.20 This arbitrariness is one of the main criticisms of absorption costing, and if absorption costing is to be used (because of its other virtues) then it is important that the methods used are kept under regular review. Changes in working conditions should, if necessary, lead to changes in the way in which work is accounted for.

5 SEPARATE DEPARTMENTAL ABSORPTION RATES
Centrally assessed 6/97

5.1 A separate absorption rate should be used for each department so that the charging of overheads will be equitable and the full cost of production items will be representative of the cost of the efforts and resources put into making them.

5.2 It is argued that if a single factory overhead absorption rate is used, some products will receive a higher overhead charge than they ought 'fairly' to bear, whereas other products will be under-charged. An example may help to illustrate this point.

Example: Separate absorption rates

5.3 Beesmore Ltd has two production departments, for which the following budgeted information is available.

	Department A	Department B	Total
Estimated overheads	£360,000	£200,000	£560,000
Estimated direct labour hours	200,000 hrs	40,000 hrs	240,000 hrs

If a single factory overhead absorption rate per direct labour hour is applied, the rate of overhead recovery would be:

$$\frac{£560,000}{240,000 \text{ hrs}} = £2.33 \text{ per direct labour hour}$$

5.4 If separate departmental rates are applied, these would be:

Department A	Department B
$\frac{£360,000}{200,000 \text{ hours}}$	$\frac{£200,000}{40,000 \text{ hours}}$
= £1.80 per direct labour hour	= £5 per direct labour hour

Department B has a higher overhead rate per hour worked than department A.

Now let us consider two separate jobs.

(a) Job X has a total direct cost of £100, takes 30 hours in department B and does not involve any work in department A.

(b) Job Y has a total direct cost of £100, takes 28 hours in department A and 2 hours in department B.

5.5 What would be the factory cost of each job, using the following rates of overhead recovery?

(a) A single factory rate of overhead recovery
(b) Separate departmental rates of overhead recovery

Solution: Separate absorption rates

		Job X £	Job Y £
5.6 (a)	*Single factory rate*		
	Direct cost	100	100
	Factory overhead (30 × £2.33)	70	70
	Factory cost	170	170
		£	£
(b)	*Separate departmental rates*		
	Direct cost	100	100.0
	Factory overhead: department A	0 (28 × 1.8)	50.4
	department B (30 × 5)	150 (2 × 5)	10.0
	Factory cost	250	160.4

5.7 Using a single factory overhead absorption rate, both jobs would cost the same. However, since job X is done entirely within department B where overhead costs are relatively higher, whereas job Y is done mostly within department A, where overhead costs are relatively lower, it is arguable that job X should cost more than job Y. This will only occur if separate departmental overhead recovery rates are used to reflect the work done on each job in each department separately.

5.8 If all jobs do not spend approximately the same time in each department then, to ensure that all jobs are charged with their fair share of overheads, it is necessary to establish separate overhead rates for each department.

6 OVER- AND UNDER-ABSORPTION

Normal costing

6.1 It was stated earlier that the usual method of accounting for overheads is to add overhead costs on the basis of a predetermined recovery rate. This rate is a sort of standard cost since it is based on figures representing what is supposed to happen (that is, figures from the budget). Using the predetermined absorption rate, the actual cost of production can be established as follows.

	Direct materials
plus:	direct labour
plus:	direct expenses
plus:	overheads (based on the predetermined overhead absorption rate)
equals:	actual cost of production

This is known as *normal costing*.

6.2 Many students become seriously confused about what can appear a very unusual method of costing (actual cost of production including a figure based on the budget). Study the following example. It will help clarify this tricky point.

Example: Normal costing

6.3 Normal Ltd budgeted to make 100 units of product Z at a cost of £3 per unit in direct materials and £4 per unit in direct labour. The sales price would be £12 per unit, and production overheads were budgeted to amount to £200. A unit basis of overhead recovery is in operation. During the period 120 units were actually produced and sold (for £12 each) and the actual cost of direct materials was £380 and of direct labour, £450. Overheads incurred came to £210.

What was the cost of sales of product Z, and what was the profit? Ignore administration, selling and distribution overheads.

Solution: Normal costing

6.4 In normal costing, the cost of production and sales is the actual direct cost plus the cost of overheads, absorbed at a predetermined rate as established in the budget. In our example, the overhead recovery rate would be £2 per unit produced (£200 ÷ 100 units).

The actual cost of sales is calculated as follows.

	£
Direct materials (actual)	380
Direct labour (actual)	450
Overheads absorbed (120 units × £2)	240
Full cost of sales, product Z	1,070
Sales of product Z (120 units × £12)	1,440
Profit, product Z	370

6.5 You may already have noticed that the actual overheads incurred, £210, are not the same as the overheads absorbed (that is, included) into the cost of production and hence charged against profit, £240; nevertheless, in normal absorption costing £240 is the 'correct' cost. The discrepancy between actual overheads incurred, and the overheads absorbed, which is an inevitable feature of normal costing, is only reconciled at the end of an accounting period, as the *under-absorption* or *over-absorption* of overhead.

Why does under- or over-absorption occur?
Centrally assessed 6/96 - 6/97

6.6 The rate of overhead absorption is based on two estimates and so it is quite likely that either one or both of the estimates will not agree with what actually occurs. Overheads incurred will, therefore, probably be either greater than or less than overheads absorbed into the cost of production. Let's consider an example.

6.7 Suppose that the estimated overhead in a production department is £80,000 and the estimated activity is 40,000 direct labour hours. The overhead recovery rate (using a direct labour hour basis) would be £2 per direct labour hour.

Actual overheads in the period are, say £84,000 and 45,000 direct labour hours are worked.

	£
Overhead incurred (actual)	84,000
Overhead absorbed (45,000 × £2)	90,000
Over-absorption of overhead	6,000

In this example, the cost of produced units or jobs has been charged with £6,000 more than was actually spent. An adjustment to reconcile the overheads charged to the actual overhead is necessary. The over-absorbed overhead will be written off as an adjustment to the profit and loss account at the end of the accounting period.

6.8 The overhead absorption rate is predetermined from estimates of overhead cost and the expected volume of activity. Under- or over-recovery of overhead will therefore occur in the following circumstances.

(a) Actual overhead costs are different from the estimates.

(b) The actual activity volume is different from the estimated activity volume.

(c) Both actual overhead costs and actual activity volume are different from the estimated costs and volume.

Example: Under/over-absorption

6.9 Only Estimates Ltd has a budgeted production overhead of £50,000 and a budgeted activity of 25,000 direct labour hours and therefore a recovery rate of £2 per direct labour hour. Calculate the under-/over-absorbed overhead, and the reasons for the under/over absorption, in the following circumstances.

(a)   Actual overheads cost £47,000 and 25,000 direct labour hours are worked.
(b)   Actual overheads cost £50,000 and 21,500 direct labour hours are worked.
(c)   Actual overheads cost £47,000 and 21,500 direct labour hours are worked.

Solution: Under/over absorption

6.10   (a)

	£
Actual overhead	47,000
Absorbed overhead (25,000 × £2)	50,000
Over-absorbed overhead	3,000

Here there is over-absorption because although the actual and estimated direct labour hours are the same, actual overheads cost *less* than expected and so too much overhead has been charged against profit.

(b)

	£
Actual overhead	50,000
Absorbed overhead (21,500 × £2)	43,000
Under-absorbed overhead	7,000

Here there is under-absorption because although estimated and actual overhead costs were the same, *fewer* direct labour hours were worked than expected and hence insufficient overheads have been charged against profit.

(c)

	£
Actual overhead	47,000
Absorbed overhead (21,500 × £2)	43,000
Under-absorbed overhead	4,000

The reason for the under-absorption is a combination of the reasons in (a) and (b).

6.11   If you are still unsure about when the overhead is under-absorbed and when it is over-absorbed try looking at it from a different point of view.

(a)   If the actual absorption rate that should have been calculated if the actual figures had been known turns out to be less than the estimated one used for absorption then too much overhead will have been absorbed: there will have been over-absorption.

(b)   If the actual rate is more than the estimated one then too little overhead will have been absorbed: there will have been under-absorption.

In summary:

Actual rate	Absorption of overheads
Less	Over
More	Under

Example: Absorption of overheads

6.12   The total production overhead expenditure of Igg Ltd, the company we encountered earlier in the chapter, was £176,533 and its actual activity was as follows.

	Machine shop A	Machine shop B	Assembly
Direct labour hours	8,200	6,500	21,900
Machine usage hours	7,300	18,700	-

Using the information in Paragraph 3.6 and the example solution in Paragraph 4.15, calculate the under-or over-absorption of overheads.

Solution: Absorption of overheads

6.13

		£	£
Actual expenditure			176,533
Overhead absorbed			
Machine shop A	7,300 hrs × £7.94	57,962	
Machine shop B	18,700 hrs × £3.50	65,450	
Assembly	21,900 hrs × £2.24	49,056	
			172,468
Under-absorbed overhead			4,065

7 PREDETERMINED RATES AND ACTUAL COSTS

7.1 Using a predetermined overhead absorption rate more often than not leads to under- or over-absorption of overheads because actual output and overhead expenditure will turn out to be different from estimated output and expenditure. You might well wonder why the complications of under- or over-absorption are necessary. Surely it would be better to use actual costs and outputs, both to avoid under- or over-absorption entirely and to obtain more 'accurate' costs of production?

7.2 Suppose that a company draws up a budget (a plan based on estimates) to make 1,200 units of a product in the *first half* of 19X5. Budgeted production overhead costs, all fixed costs, are £12,000. Due to seasonal demand for the company's product, the volume of production varies from month to month. Actual overhead costs are £2,000 per month. Actual monthly production in the first half of 19X5 is listed below, and total actual production in the period is 1,080 units.

The table below shows the production overhead cost per unit using the following.

(a) A predetermined absorption rate of $\dfrac{£12,000}{1,200}$ = £10 per unit

(b) An actual overhead cost per unit each month

(c) An actual overhead cost per unit based on actual six-monthly expenditure of £12,000 and actual six-monthly output of 1,080 units = £11.11 per unit

			Overhead cost per unit		
			(a)	*(b)*	*(c)*
			Predetermined	*Actual cost*	*Average actual cost*
	Expenditure	*Output*	*unit rate*	*each month*	*in the six months*
Month	*(A)*	*(B)*		*(A) ÷ (B)*	
	£	Units	£	£	£
Jan	2,000	100	10	20.00	11.11
Feb	2,000	120	10	16.67	11.11
Mar	2,000	140	10	14.29	11.11
April	2,000	160	10	12.50	11.11
May	2,000	320	10	6.25	11.11
June	2,000	240	10	8.33	11.11
	12,000	1,080			

7.3 Methods (a) and (c) give a constant overhead cost per unit each month, regardless of seasonal variations in output. Method (b) gives variable unit overhead costs, depending on the time of the year. For this reason, it is argued that method (a) or (c) would provide more useful (long-term) costing information.

7.4 In addition, if prices are based on full cost with a percentage mark-up for profit, method (b) would give seasonal variations in selling prices, with high prices in low-season and low prices in high-season. Methods (a) and (c) would give a constant price based on 'cost plus'.

7.5   With method (a), overhead costs per unit are known throughout the period, and cost statements can be prepared at any time. This is because predetermined overhead rates are known in advance. With method (c), overhead costs cannot be established until after the end of the accounting period. For example, overhead costs of output in January 19X5 cannot be established until actual costs and output for the period are known, which will be not until after the end of June 19X5.

7.6   For the reasons given above, predetermined overhead rates are preferable to actual overhead costs, in spite of being estimates of costs and in spite of the need to write off under-or over-absorbed overhead costs to the P & L account.

8   FIXED AND VARIABLE OVERHEADS AND CAPACITY

8.1   When an organisation has estimated fixed and variable production overheads, it may calculate a separate absorption rate for each.

(a)   A fixed overhead absorption rate is intended to share out a fixed cost for a given time period between items of production (or other activities).

(b)   A variable overhead absorption rate is intended to charge a variable cost to the item of production (or other activity) that is responsible for incurring the cost. Extra activity adds to the total variable overhead cost, and the variable overhead absorption rate is intended to recognise this fact.

8.2   For example, suppose that a company expects its fixed overhead costs in period 8 to be £12,000 and its variable overhead costs to be £1 per direct labour hour.

(a)   If the budget is for 4,000 direct labour hours, the absorption rate per hour would be as follows.

	£
Fixed overhead (£12,000 ÷ 4,000)	3
Variable overhead	1
Total	4

(b)   If the budget is for 5,000 direct labour hours, the absorption rate per hour would be as follows.

	£
Fixed overhead (£12,000 ÷ 5,000)	2.4
Variable overhead	1.0
Total	3.4

The absorption rate, and so the fully absorbed cost of production, comes down as the budgeted volume of activity rises, but only for fixed overheads, not variable overheads. This is because the (constant) fixed overheads are being shared between a greater number of hours whereas the total variable overhead continues to rise with the volume of activity.

Overhead absorption rates, costs and capacity

8.3   The importance of the volume of activity in absorption costing cannot be overstated, not only because large differences between budgeted and actual volume create large amounts of under- or over-absorbed overheads, but also because higher budgeted output reduces absorption rates and costs.

8.4   A major criticism of absorption costing derives from this point. We saw when discussing materials that the modern view is that production should be tailored to demand. Under absorption costing however, managers are tempted to produce, not for the market, but to absorb allocated overheads and reduce unit costs. Production in excess of demand, however, really only increases the overheads (for example warehousing) that the organisation has to bear.

Full capacity, practical capacity and budgeted capacity

8.5 In connection with capacity you may come across a number of terms, as follows.

(a) *Full capacity* is the maximum number of hours that could be worked in ideal conditions.

(b) *Practical capacity* is full capacity less an allowance for hours lost unavoidably because conditions are not ideal.

(c) *Budgeted capacity* is the number of hours that a business plans to work.

As a simple example, budgeted capacity would be 60% of practical capacity if a business planned to work a 3 day week rather than a 5 day week. Full capacity would be a 7 day week.

9 ACTIVITY BASED COSTING
Centrally assessed 6/96

Overheads and the current industrial environment

9.1 Absorption costing appears to be a relatively straightforward way of adding overhead costs to units of production using, more often than not, a volume-related absorption basis (such as direct labour hours or direct machine hours). The assumption that all overheads are related primarily to production volume is therefore implied in an absorption costing system.

9.2 Nowadays, however, with the advent of advanced manufacturing technology, overheads are likely to be a very important part of cost and hence errors in adding overheads can be significant.

9.3 There has also been an increase in what are termed service support functions, such as setting-up, production scheduling, first item inspection and data processing. These overheads are not, however, greatly affected by changes in production volume. They tend to vary according to the range and complexity of the products manufactured rather than the volume of output.

9.4 To reflect this change in circumstances an alternative method of accounting for overheads called activity based costing (ABC) has been developed.

The ideas behind ABC

9.5 The major ideas behind ABC are as follows.

(a) Activities cause costs.

Activities include ordering, materials handling, machining, assembly, production scheduling and despatching.

(b) Products create demand for these activities.

(c) Overhead costs are assigned to a product on the basis of a product's consumption of the activities.

Outline of an ABC system

9.6 An ABC system operates as follows.

(a) *Step 1*

Identify an organisation's major activities.

(b) *Step 2*

Identify the factors which determine how large the costs associated with an activity will be. The factors are known as *cost drivers*. Look at the following examples.

Activity	Possible cost driver
Setting-up	Number of production runs
Production scheduling	Number of production runs
Materials handling	Number of production runs
Inspection	Number of inspections, inspection hours or production runs
Raw materials inventory handling	Number of purchase orders delivered
Finished goods inventory handling and despatch	Number of customer orders delivered

There are, of course, some costs (short-term variable costs) that do vary with production levels in the short term and ABC still uses volume-related cost drivers such as labour or machine hours for these costs. The cost of oil used as a lubricant on machines would be added to products on the basis of the number of machine hours since oil would have to be used for each hour that the machines ran.

(c) *Step 3*

Collect the costs associated with each cost driver into what are known as cost pools Thus in our example all the costs involved in production runs will be collected in one cost pool, all the costs involved in inspections in another and so on.

A value per cost driver is then calculated as $\dfrac{\text{costs of cost pool}}{\text{number of associated cost driver}}$. For production runs this would be $\dfrac{\text{total costs of production runs}}{\text{number of production runs}}$.

(d) *Step 4*

Charge overheads to products on the basis of the number of each cost driver the product requires. A batch of 10,000 units requiring five production runs would therefore have to bear the following proportion of the overhead costs driven by production runs:

5 × (value per production run cost driver).

9.7   Let's look at an example to see how ABC works in practice.

Example: Activity based costing

9.8   A company manufactures two products, L and M, using the same equipment and similar processes. An extract of the production data for these products in one period is shown below.

	L	M
Quantity produced (units)	5,000	7,000
Direct labour hours per unit	1	2
Machine hours per unit	3	1
Set-ups in the period	10	40
Orders handled in the period	15	60

Overhead costs	£
Relating to machine activity	220,000
Relating to production run set-ups	20,000
Relating to handling of orders	45,000
	285,000

Calculate the production overhead to be assigned to one unit of each of the products using the following costing methods.

(a) A traditional absorption costing approach using a direct labour hour rate to absorb overheads

(b) An activity based costing approach, using suitable cost drivers to trace overheads to products

Solution: Activity based costing

9.9 (a)

		Direct labour hours
Product L = 5,000 units × 1 hour		5,000
Product M = 7,000 units × 2 hours		14,000
		19,000

$$\therefore \text{ Overhead absorption rate } = \frac{£285,000}{19,000}$$

$$= £15 \text{ per hour}$$

Overhead absorbed would be as follows.

Product L	1 hour × £15	=	£15 per unit
Product M	2 hours × £15	=	£30 per unit

(b)

		Machine hours
Product L	= 5,000 units × 3 hours	15,000
Product M	= 7,000 units × 1 hour	7,000
		22,000

Using ABC the overhead costs are charged according to the cost drivers.

	£		
Machine-hour driven costs	220,000	÷ 22,000 m/c hours	= £10 per m/c hour
Set-up driven costs	20,000	÷ 50 set ups	= £400 per set up
Order-driven costs	45,000	÷ 75 orders	= £600 per order

Overhead costs are therefore as follows.

		Product L £		Product M £
Machine-driven costs	(15,000 hrs × £10)	150,000	(7,000 hrs × £10)	70,000
Set-up costs	(10 × £400)	4,000	(40 × £400)	16,000
Order-handling costs	(15 × £600)	9,000	(60 × £600)	36,000
		163,000		122,000
Units produced		5,000		7,000
Overhead cost per unit		£32.60		£17.43

9.10 These figures suggest that product M absorbs an unrealistic amount of overhead using a direct labour hour basis. Overhead cost per unit should be based on the factors which drive the costs, in this case machine hours, the number of production run set-ups and the number of orders handled for each product. Advocates of ABC argue that the resulting product costs will be more relevant for management planning and decision making.

Example: ABC

9.11 Suppose that Cooplan Ltd manufactures four products, W, X, Y and Z. Output and cost data for the period just ended are as follows.

	Output	Number of production runs in the period	Material cost per unit	Direct labour hours per unit	Machine hours per unit
	Units		£		
W	10	2	20	1	1
X	10	2	80	3	3
Y	100	5	20	1	1
Z	100	5	80	3	3
		14			

Direct labour cost per hour is £5. Overhead costs are as follows.

	£
Short-run variable costs	3,080
Set-up costs	10,920
Expediting and scheduling costs	9,100
Materials handling costs	7,700
	30,800

What would be the cost of one unit of each of the four products using ABC?

Solution: ABC

9.12 We assume that the number of production runs is the cost driver for set-up costs, expediting and scheduling costs and materials handling costs and that machine hours are the cost driver for short-run variable costs. Unit costs are therefore calculated as follows.

	W	X	Y	Z	Total
	£	£	£	£	£
Direct material	200	800	2,000	8,000	11,000
Direct labour	50	150	500	1,500	2,200
Short-run variable overheads (W1)	70	210	700	2,100	3,080
Set-up costs (W2)	1,560	1,560	3,900	3,900	10,920
Expediting, scheduling costs (W3)	1,300	1,300	3,250	3,250	9,100
Materials handling costs (W4)	1,100	1,100	2,750	2,750	7,700
	4,280	5,120	13,100	21,500	44,000

	W	X	Y	Z
	£	£	£	£
Units produced	10	10	100	100
Cost per unit	£428	£512	£131	£215

Workings

1	£3,080 ÷ 440 machine hours =	=	£7 per machine hour
2	£10,920 ÷ 14 production runs	=	£780 per run
3	£9,100 ÷ 14 production runs	=	£650 per run
4	£7,700 ÷ 14 production runs	=	£550 per run

Advantages of ABC

9.13 ABC is a fairly new technique and continues to increase in popularity. Experts are divided on the extent to which ABC will replace more traditional costing methods but many believe that it does have certain advantages over absorption costing.

(a) Absorption costing usually uses two absorption bases (labour hours and/or machine hours) to charge overheads to products whereas ABC uses many different cost drivers as absorption bases. Rates under ABC should therefore be more closely linked to the causes of overhead costs and hence should produce more realistic product costs, especially where support overheads are high.

(b) Focusing attention on what actually causes overheads and tracing overheads to products on the basis of cost driver usage ensures that a greater proportion of overheads are product related. Absorption costing, on the other hand, does seem to relate overheads to products in a very arbitrary way. It is claimed that it is this feature of ABC which produces more accurate product costs. In turn pricing policy should reflect this. Focusing attention on the causes of overheads can also help in their control

---

Key points in this chapter

- Absorption costing charges a share of all overheads to products. It is used for stock valuation, for pricing decisions and to compare the profitability of different products.

- The three stages of absorption costing are allocation, apportionment and absorption.

- Apportionment involves sharing costs out amongst different departments or cost centres.

- Absorption involves adding the costs that have been shared out to the cost of cost units. This is done according to a predetermined rate found by dividing total estimated overheads by the total estimated quantity of the basis of absorption.

- Separate absorption rates should be used for each production department to ensure fairness.

- Over-absorption occurs when the estimated absorption rate is too high.

- Under-absorption occurs when the estimated absorption rate is too low.

- A predetermined rate is used to ensure a constant overhead cost per unit, to avoid fluctuations in selling prices and for administrative convenience.

- Separate rates may be calculated for fixed and variable overheads. For fixed overheads the absorption rate falls as the volume of production (or 'capacity') rises.

- Activity based costing is a recent development which appears to be less arbitrary than absorption costing.

For practice on the points covered in this chapter you should now attempt the Exercises in Session 5 of the Cost Information Workbook

Part B
Bookeeping entries for cost information

6 Bookkeeping entries for cost information

This chapter covers the following topics.

1   Cost information and ledger accounting

2   Getting costs into finished units

3   Control accounts

4   Bookkeeping systems

---

1   COST INFORMATION AND LEDGER ACCOUNTING

1.1   In the previous chapters we have scrupulously avoided T accounts, debits and credits, ledgers and bookkeeping. The cost records we have described so far are quite adequate for individual products or jobs, and it is not essential to go beyond this.

1.2   However, unless records of *totals* are maintained and checks of these records are made, there is no way of knowing whether all the costs that should have been recorded really have been recorded. The solution to this problem is to link the cost records to the cash and credit transactions that are summarised in the nominal ledger. If you like you can think of recording cost information as *dealing with debits*. Let us look at an example to illustrate what we mean.

Example: Cost information and ledger accounting

1.3   Suppose you buy £100 of materials for cash and £100 on credit. What entries will you make in the ledgers?

1.4   From the knowledge you have already acquired elsewhere you should have no difficulty in answering this question. The cash transaction will be recorded in the cash book, analysed as appropriate. It will also be recorded in the nominal ledger as follows.

		£	£
DEBIT	Purchases	100	
CREDIT	Cash		100

1.5   The credit transaction will be recorded in the purchase day book and then in the purchase ledger under the name of the supplier in question. It will also be recorded in the nominal ledger as follows.

		£	£
DEBIT	Purchases	100	
CREDIT	Creditors ledger control account		100

1.6   Now consider this transaction from the point of view of what you have learnt in this book. The appropriate stores ledger and bin card will have been updated to show the acquisition of £200 worth of stock but the cash and credit side of the transactions have not entered any cost records. In other words, the cost records are only interested in the entry made in the nominal ledger under purchases.

1.7   We could go further and explain that just as the analysed cash book is a very detailed breakdown of the entries in the cash control account in the nominal ledger, and just as the creditors ledger shows the detailed information behind the creditors ledger control account, the cost records are a detailed breakdown of the information contained in the purchases account, the wages and salaries account, and all the expense accounts in the nominal ledger.

1.8   It is tempting to go no further than this. So long as you understand the basic principles of double entry bookkeeping, the cost accounting aspects of it should cause you no more difficulty than any other aspects.

1.9   All you really need to know, however, is the following.

   (a) How to turn purchases, wages and so on into finished units of production.
   (b) How to deal with under-/or over-absorbed overheads
   (c) How to deal with variances (covered in chapter 9).

2   GETTING COSTS INTO FINISHED UNITS

2.1   In your studies for other Units you may have come across 'stock' accounts, and you may have got used to the idea that entries are only made in these accounts at the year end (the opening stock balance is written off to the profit and loss account and the closing stock balance is carried forward in its place). The following layout should be very familiar.

	P & L	
	£	£
Sales		3,600
Opening stock	500	
Materials	500	
Labour	500	
Production overheads	500	
	2,000	
Closing stock	(200)	
Cost of sales		(1,800)
Gross profit		1,800

2.2   The confusing thing here is that there are three figures that represent stock, but only two that are bold enough to advertise the fact! The figure called 'cost of sales' is, of course, stock that has been sold.

2.3   We shall demonstrate how a single purchase of materials works through into the final accounts. The relevant double entries are:

			£	£
(a)	DEBIT	Materials	X	
	CREDIT	Cash		X

Being the buying of materials which are put into raw materials stock

			£	£
(b)	DEBIT	Work in progress	X	
	CREDIT	Materials		X

Being the issue of materials to production for use in work in progress

			£	£
(c)	DEBIT	Finished goods	X	
	CREDIT	Work in progress		X

Being the issue of units that are now finished to finished goods stock

			£	£
(d)	DEBIT	Cost of sales	X	
	CREDIT	Finished goods		X

Being the taking of units out of finished goods stock and selling them

			£	£
(e)	DEBIT	Profit and loss account	X	
	CREDIT	Cost of sales		X

Being the closing off of ledger accounts and the drawing up of financial statements

2.4   Entry (e) would only be made at the end of a period.

Example: Basic cost accounting entries

2.5   Sun Dried Tomatoes Ltd begins trading with £20 cash. It buys £20 of tomatoes and puts £10 worth in the fridge and the other £10 out in the sun. Before long £5 worth are ready and are duly sold for £15. How will these events and transactions be reflected in the books?

Solution: Basic cost accounting entries

		Dr £	Cr £
	Cash		
Cash - opening balance		20	
Purchase of materials			20
Sale of finished goods		15	
Closing balance			15
		35	35
	Materials		
Cash purchase		20	
Transfer to WIP			10
Closing balance			10
		20	20
	Work in progress		
Transfer from materials		10	
Transfer to finished goods			5
Closing balance			5
		10	10
	Finished goods		
Transfer from WIP		5	
Transfer to cost of sales			5
		5	5
	Cost of sales		
Transfer from finished goods		5	
Shown in profit and loss account			5
		5	5
	Sales		
Shown in profit and loss account		15	
Cash			15
		15	15

SUNDRIED TOMATOES LTD
PROFIT AND LOSS ACCOUNT

	£
Sales	15
Cost of sales	5
Profit	10

SUNDRIED TOMATOES LTD
BALANCE SHEET

		£	£
Cash			15
Stocks:	materials	10	
	WIP	5	
			15
			30
Capital:	b/f		20
	profit		10
			30

2.7 The principle, as you can see, is very straightforward. We have not included entries for labour costs or direct expenses to keep things simple, but these are treated in the same way. Instead of amounts being debited initially to the materials account, they would be debited to the labour costs or direct expenses accounts (with cash being credited). They would then be transferred to work in progress and the other entries would be as for materials. Overheads are slightly more (but not much more) problematic.

Dealing with overheads
Centrally assessed 6/96

2.8 When an absorption costing system is in use we now know that the amount of overhead included in the cost of an item is absorbed at a predetermined rate. The entries made in the cash book and the nominal ledger, however, are the actual amounts.

2.9 As we saw in the previous chapter, it is highly unlikely that the actual amount and the predetermined amount will be the same. The difference is called under- or over-absorbed overhead. To deal with this in the cost accounting books, therefore, we need to have an account to collect under- or over-absorbed amounts for each type of overhead.

Example: The under-/over-absorbed overhead account

2.10 Danquayle Potatoes Ltd absorbs production overheads at the rate of £0.50 per operating hour and administration overheads at 20% of the production cost of sales. Actual data for one month was as follows.

Administration overheads	£32,000
Production overheads	£46,500
Operating hours	90,000
Production cost of sales	£180,000

What entries need to be made for overheads in the ledgers?

Solution: The under-/over-absorbed overhead account

2.11

	Dr £	Cr £
Production overheads		
Cash	46,500	
Absorbed into WIP (90,000 × £0.50)		45,000
Under-absorbed overhead		1,500
	46,500	46,500
Administration overheads		
Cash	32,000	
To cost of sales (180,000 × 0.2)		36,000
Over-absorbed overhead	4,000	
	36,000	36,000
Under-/over-absorbed overhead		
Production overhead	1,500	
Administration overhead		4,000
Balance to profit and loss account	2,500	
	4,000	4,000

2.12 *Less* production overhead has been absorbed than has been spent so there is under-absorbed overhead of £1,500; more administration overhead has been absorbed (into cost of sales, note, not into WIP) and so there is over-absorbed overhead of £4,000. The net over-absorbed overhead of £2,500 is a credit in the profit and loss account.

3 CONTROL ACCOUNTS

Centrally assessed 12/95

Control accounts

3.1 Obviously the previous section is highly simplified: this is to avoid obscuring the basic principles. For example, we have until now assumed that if £200 of materials are purchased the only entries made will be Dr Materials, Cr Cash. In practice, of course, this £200 might be made up of 20 different types of material, each costing £10, and if so each type of material is likely to have its own sub-account. These sub-accounts would be exactly like individual personal accounts in the creditors ledger or the debtors ledger. You have probably guessed that we need to use *control accounts* to summarise the detailed transactions (such as how the £200 of materials is made up) and to maintain the double entry in the nominal ledger.

(a) A *materials control account* (or *stores control account*) records the total cost of invoices received for each type of material (purchases) and the total cost of each type of material issued to various departments (the sum of the value of all materials requisition notes).

(b) A *wages control account* records the total cost of the payroll (plus employer's national insurance contributions) and the total cost of direct and indirect labour as recorded in the wages analysis sheets and charged to each production job or process.

(c) A *production overhead control account* is a total record of actual expenditure incurred and the amount absorbed into individual units, jobs or processes. Subsidiary records for actual overhead expenditure items and cost records which show the overheads attributed to individual units or jobs must agree with or reconcile to the totals in the control account.

(d) A *work in progress control account* records the total costs of direct materials, direct wages and production overheads charged to units, jobs or processes, and the cost of finished goods which are completed and transferred to the distribution department. Subsidiary records of individual job costs and so on will exist for jobs still in production and for jobs completed.

3.2 The precise level of detail depends entirely upon the individual organisation. For example an organisation that makes different products might want a hierarchy of materials accounts as follows.

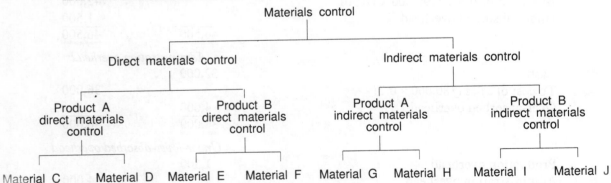

Coding

3.3 Each account in use needs to be classified by the use of coding. A suggested computer-based four-digit numerical coding account system is set out below.

Basic structure	Code number	Allocation
(a) First division	1000 – 4999	This range provides for cost accounts and is divided into four main departmental sections with ten cost centre subsections in each department, allowing for a maximum of 99 accounts in each cost centre
Second division	1000 – 1999 2000 – 2999 3000 – 3999 4000 – 4999	Departments 1 to 4
Third division	000 – 099 100 – 199 200 – 299 and so on	Facility for ten cost centres in each department
Fourth division		Breakdown of costs in each cost centre
	01 – 39	direct costs
	40 – 79	indirect costs
	80 – 99	spare capacity
(b)	5000 – 5999	This range provides for the following. (i) Revenue accounts (ii) Work in progress accounts (iii) Finished goods accounts (iv) Cost of sales accounts (v) General expenses accounts (vi) Profit and loss account
(c)	6000 – 6999	This range provides for individual stores items
(d)	7000 – 7999	This range provides for individual debtor accounts
(e)	8000 – 8999	This range provides for individual creditor accounts
(f)	9000 – 9999	This range is used for balance sheet accounts including the following. (i) Stores control account (ii) Debtors' control account (iii) Creditors' control account

3.4 An illustration of the coding of direct labour (grade T) might be as follows.

Department 2

Cost centre	*1*	*2*	*3*	*4*
Direct labour (grade T)	2009	2109	2209	2309

3.5 The four digit code is explained as follows.

(a) The first digit, 2, refers to department 2.
(b) The second digit 0, 1, 2 or 3 refers to the cost centre which incurred the cost.
(c) The last two digits, 09, refer to 'direct labour costs, grade T'.

3.6 Obviously systems that you come across in practice will exhibit different features. The above describes only broad characteristics that are likely to be typical of all such systems.

4   BOOKKEEPING SYSTEMS

4.1   You may encounter the terms 'interlocking accounts' and 'integrated accounts', but in practice you are far more likely to deal only with integrated systems and therefore this is the system we will describe. Briefly, the difference between the two systems is that interlocking systems require separate ledgers to be kept for the cost accounting function and the financial accounting function, whereas integrated systems combine the two functions in one set of ledger accounts.

An integrated system

4.2   Integrated accounts are what we were describing in the earlier parts of this chapter. The following diagram provides an overview of a basic system of integrated accounts. Simplifications as to entries in the individual accounts have, of course, been made but study the diagram carefully. Work through the double entries represented in the diagram and make sure that you understand the logic behind them.

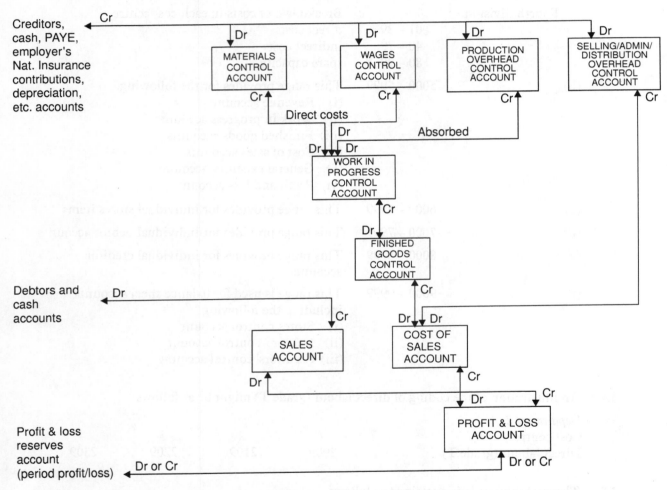

4.3   Having digested the information contained in the diagram, the best way of continuing is to give a full example.

Example: Integrated accounts

4.4   Shown below are the opening balances for the month of October 19X2 with respect to Integra Products Ltd, with a summary bank account and information obtained from the stores department, the payroll department and the production department. The provisions for depreciation have been decided, but the double entry has not been completed. During the month £196,000 worth of goods were sold (all on credit) for £278,000.

The information given has to be posted to the integrated accounts and a trading and profit and loss account has to be prepared for October 19X2. A trial balance as at 31 October 19X2 has also to be drawn up.

STORES REPORT - OCTOBER 19X2

	£'000
Materials received from suppliers and invoiced	40
Materials issued to production	32
Materials issued to production service departments	8
Materials issued to administrative departments	2

PAYROLL REPORT - OCTOBER 19X2

	Gross wages £'000	PAYE & employees' NI £'000	Net £'000	Employer's NI £'000
Direct wages (£5.50 per hour)	33	8	25	2
Production indirect wages	7	1	6	-
Administrative staff wages and salaries	10	3	7	1
Selling staff wages and salaries	10	3	7	1
	60	15	45	4

PRODUCTION REPORT - OCTOBER 19X2

Production overhead absorption rate:	£12.50 per direct labour hour
Value of work completed in the month:	£150,000

CASH AND BANK ACCOUNT

	£'000		£'000
Debtors	290	Balance b/f	50
		Wages and salaries	45
		Production overhead	15
		Administration overhead	8
		Selling overhead	20
		Creditors for national insurance and PAYE	19
		Creditors	45
		Balance c/f (surplus)	88
	290		290
Balance b/f	88		

RAW MATERIALS STORES ACCOUNT

	£'000		£'000
Balance b/f	30	Work in progress	32
Creditors	40	Production overhead	8
		Administration overhead	2
		Balance c/f	28
	70		70
Balance b/f	28		

WAGES AND SALARIES ACCOUNT

	£'000		£'000
Bank	45	Work in progress	33
Creditor for national insurance		Production overhead	7
and PAYE	15	Administration overhead	10
		Selling overhead	10
	60		60

PRODUCTION OVERHEAD ACCOUNT

	£'000		£'000
Raw materials stores	8	Work in progress	75
Wages and salaries	7		
Bank (expenses)	15		
Depreciation: buildings	2		
Depreciation: equipment	35		
Over-absorbed overhead (bal fig)	8		
	75		75

WORK IN PROGRESS ACCOUNT

	£'000		£'000
Balance b/f	20	Finished goods	150
Raw materials stores	32		
Wages and salaries	33		
Creditors for national insurance	2		
Production overhead	75	Balance c/f	12
	162		162
Balance b/f	12		

FINISHED GOODS ACCOUNT

	£'000		£'000
Balance b/f	60	Cost of sales	196
Work in progress	150	Balance c/f	14
	210		210
Balance b/f	14		

COST OF SALES ACCOUNT

	£'000		£'000
Finished goods	196	Profit and loss account	196

ADMINISTRATION OVERHEAD ACCOUNT

	£'000		£'000
Raw materials stores	2	Profit and loss account	26
Wages and salaries	10		
Bank (expenses)	8		
Creditor for national insurance	1		
Depreciation	5		
	26		26

SELLING OVERHEAD ACCOUNT

	£'000		£'000
Wages and salaries	10	Profit and loss account	31
Bank (expenses)	20		
Creditor for national insurance	1		
	31		31

UNDER-/OVER-ABSORBED OVERHEAD ACCOUNT

	£'000		£'000
Profit and loss account	8	Production overhead account	8

SALES ACCOUNT

	£'000		£'000
Profit and loss account	278	Debtors	278

TRADING AND PROFIT AND LOSS ACCOUNT

	£'000		£'000
Cost of sales	196	Sales	278
Gross profit c/d	82		
	278		278
Administration overhead	26	Gross profit b/d	82
Selling overhead	31	Over-absorbed overhead	8
Profit and loss reserves	33		
	90		90

DEBTORS ACCOUNT

	£'000		£'000
Balance b/f	74	Bank	290
Sales	278	Balance c/f	62
	352		352
Balance b/f	62		

CREDITORS ACCOUNT

	£'000		£'000
Bank	45	Balance b/f	85
Balance c/f	80	Raw materials stores	40
	125		125
		Balance b/f	80

CREDITOR FOR NATIONAL INSURANCE & PAYE

	£'000		£'000
Bank	19	Balance b/f	19
		Wages and salaries	15
Balance c/f	19	Employer's contributions:	
		Work in progress	2
		Administration overhead	1
		Selling overhead	1
	38		38
		Balance b/f	19

FACTORY BUILDINGS ACCOUNT

	£'000		£'000
Balance b/f	250	Balance c/f	250

PROVISION FOR DEPRECIATION: FACTORY AND BUILDINGS

	£'000		£'000
Balance c/f	22	Balance b/f	20
		Charge for October 19X2	2
	22		22
		Balance b/f	22

EQUIPMENT ACCOUNT

	£'000		£'000
Balance b/f	320	Balance c/f	320

PROVISION FOR DEPRECIATION: EQUIPMENT

	£'000		£'000
Balance c/f	210	Balance b/f	170
		Factory equipment charge	35
		Office equipment charge	5
	210		210
		Balance b/f	210

SHARE CAPITAL ACCOUNT

	£'000		£'000
Balance c/f	100	Balance b/f	100

SHARE PREMIUM ACCOUNT

	£'000		£'000
Balance c/f	20	Balance b/f	20

PROFIT AND LOSS RESERVES

	£'000		£'000
Balance c/f	323	Balance b/f	290
		Profit and loss account	33
	323		323
		Balance b/f	323

The trial balance as at 31 October 19X2 is as follows.

	DR		CR
	£'000		£'000
Raw materials stores	28	Creditors	80
Work in progress	12	Creditor for national insurance	
Finished goods	14	and PAYE	19
Cash and bank	88	Provision for depreciation:	
Debtors	62	Factory and buildings	22
Factory and buildings	250	Equipment	210
Equipment	320	Share capital	100
		Share premium	20
		Profit and loss reserves	323
	774		774

4.5 The amount of production overhead transferred to WIP is calculated by multiplying the rate given (£12.50 per direct labour hour) by the number of direct labour hours, which was £33,000/£5.50 = 6,000.

$$£12.50 \times 6,000 = £75,000$$

4.6 We are not told that administration and selling overheads are absorbed into units produced, so we must assume that the actual costs are charged in full in the period in which they are incurred. A 'vertical' profit and loss account may make this clearer.

	£'000	£'000
Sales		278
Opening stocks (30 + 20 + 60)	110	
Direct materials purchased (40 – 8 – 2)	30	
Wages and salaries (33 + 2)	35	
Production overhead	75	
	250	
Closing stocks (28 + 12 + 14)	(54)	
Cost of sales		196
Gross profit		82
Administration overhead	26	
Selling overhead	31	
Over-absorbed overhead	(8)	
		(49)
Net profit		33

Key points in this chapter

- The bookkeeping aspects of recording cost information are quite straightforward.

- Direct expenses and overheads are collected in the WIP control account and the total is transferred to finished goods.

- An under-/over-absorbed overhead account is needed if actual overheads are different from those budgeted.

- Control accounts are used to summarise detailed transactions.

- Modern (computerised) systems integrate cost information and financial accounting information in one set of accounts (integrated system). Older systems used separate ledgers for financial accounts and cost accounts (interlocking system).

For practice on the points covered in this chapter you should now attempt the Exercises in Session 6 of the Cost Information Workbook

Part C
Costing methods

7 Job, batch and process costing

This chapter covers the following topics.

1 What is a costing method?

2 Job costing

3 An illustration of job costing

4 Batch costing

5 What is process costing?

6 The aims of process costing

7 Accounting for waste or loss

8 Partly completed output

9 Joint products and by-products

---

1   WHAT IS A COSTING METHOD?

1.1   A costing method is a method of collecting costs which is designed to suit the way goods are processed or manufactured or the way that services are provided. Each organisation's costing method will therefore have unique features but costing systems of firms in the same line of business will more than likely have common aspects. On the other hand, organisations involved in completely different activities, such as hospitals and car part manufacturers, will use very different costing methods.

2   JOB COSTING
Centrally assessed 12/95, 6/96 and 6/97

2.1   The aim of job costing is simply to collect the cost information shown below.

	£
Materials	X
Labour	X
Expenses	X
Direct cost	X
Production overhead	X
Total production cost	X
Administration overhead	X
Selling overhead	X
Cost of sales	X

To the final figure is added a 'mark-up' and the total is the selling price of the job.

2.2   In other words, all we are doing is looking at one way of putting together the pieces of information that we have studied separately so far.

What is a job?

2.3   A job is a cost unit which consists of a single order or contract. With other methods of costing it is usual to produce for stock; this means that the management decide in advance how many units of each type, size, colour, quality and so on will be produced during the coming year regardless of the identity of the customers who will eventually buy the products. In job costing, on the other hand, production is usually carried out in accordance with the special requirements of each customer. It is therefore usual for each job to differ in one or more respects from every other job, which means that a separate record must be maintained to show the details of a particular job.

Procedure for the performance of jobs

2.4   The normal procedure which is adopted in jobbing concerns involves the following.

(a)   The prospective customer approaches the supplier and discusses the precise details of the items to be supplied, for example the quantity, quality, size and colour of the goods, the date of delivery and any special requirements.

(b)   The estimating department of the organisation then prepares an estimate for the job. This will include the cost of the materials to be used, the wages to be paid, the appropriate amount for overhead, the cost (where appropriate) of additional equipment needed specially for the job, and finally the supplier's profit margin. The total of these items will represent the quoted selling price.

(c)   At the appropriate time, the job will be 'loaded' on to the factory floor. This means that as soon as all materials, labour and equipment are available and subject to the scheduling of other orders, the job will be started.

Collection of job costs

2.5 Materials requisitions are sent to stores. The materials requisition note will be used to cost the materials issued to the job concerned, and this cost may then be recorded on a *job cost sheet* or *job cost card*. The cost may include items already in stock, at an appropriate valuation, and/or items specially purchased. An example of a job cost card is shown on the following page.

2.6 A job card or job ticket is completed by the worker who is to perform the first operation. The times of his starting and finishing the operation are recorded on the card, which may then be passed to the person who is to carry out the second operation.

2.7 Alternatively each worker may complete a separate card. When the job is completed, the job cards are sent to the cost office, where the time spent will be costed and recorded on the job cost sheet. (An example of a job card is shown in Chapter 3.)

2.8 The relevant costs of materials issued, direct labour performed and direct expenses incurred as recorded on the job cost card are charged to the job account which will be a sub-account of the work in progress control account. The total of the balances on the job accounts will equal the balance on the work in progress control account.

2.9 The job account is debited with the job's share of the production overhead, based on the absorption rate(s) in operation. If the job is incomplete at the end of an accounting period, it is valued at factory cost in the closing balance sheet (if a system of absorption costing, as previously described in this Tutorial Text, is in operation).

2.10 On completion of the job, the job account may be charged with the appropriate administration, selling and distribution overhead, after which the total cost of the job can be ascertained.

JOB ACCOUNT

	£		£
Materials issued	X	Finished jobs	X
Direct labour	X		
Direct expenses	X		
Factory overhead at predetermined rate	X		
Other overheads	X		X
	X		X

2.11 The difference between the agreed selling price and the total actual cost will be the supplier's profit (or loss).

2.12 Once jobs are complete, job cost cards are transferred from the work in progress category to finished goods. When delivery is made to the customer, the costs become a cost of sale. If the completed job was carried out in order to build up finished goods stocks (rather than to meet a specific order) the quantity of items produced and their value are recorded on finished goods stores ledger cards.

JOB COST CARD

Job No.	

Customer	Customer's Order No.	Start Date
Job Description		Delivery Date
Estimate Ref.	Invoice No.	
Quoted price	Invoice price	Despatch Note No.

Material						Labour								Overheads			
Date	Req. No.	Qty.	Price	Cost		Date	Lab Anal Ref.	Cost Ctre	Hrs.	Rate	Bonus	Cost		Hrs	OAR	Cost	
				£	p							£	p			£	p
Total C/F						Total C/F								Total C/F			

Expenses					Job Cost Summary	Actual		Estimate	
						£	p	£	p
Date	Ref.	Description	Cost						
			£	p					
					Direct Materials B/F				
					Direct Expenses B/F				
					Direct Labour B/F				
					= Prime Cost				
					Factory Overheads B/F				
					= Factory Cost				
					Selling & Admin. Overheads				
					% on Factory Cost				
					= Total Cost				
					Invoice Price				
Total C/F					Job Profit/Loss				

Comments

Job Cost Card Completed by ....

Rectification costs

2.13 Sometimes when the finished output is inspected it is found to be sub-standard. It may be possible to rectify the fault, so the sub-standard output will be returned to the department or cost centre where the fault arose. The costs arising from this are called *rectification costs* and you should know how to deal with such costs in a job costing system.

2.14 Rectification costs can be treated in two ways, depending on the circumstances in which the costs have arisen.

(a) If rectification work is not a frequent occurrence, but arises on occasions with specific jobs to which it can be traced directly, then the rectification costs should be charged as a direct cost to the jobs concerned.

(b) If rectification is regarded as a normal part of the work carried out generally in the department, then the rectification costs should be treated as production overheads. This means that they would be included in the total of production overheads for the department and absorbed into the cost of all jobs for the period, using the overhead absorption rate.

Job costing and computerisation

2.15 Job costing cards or sheets exist in manual systems, but it is increasingly likely the job costing system will be computerised, using specifically designed accounting software. A computerised job accounting system is likely to contain the following features.

(a) Every job will be given a job code number, which will determine how the data relating to the job is stored.

(b) A separate set of codes will be given for the type of costs that any job is likely to incur. Thus, 'direct wages', say, will have the same code whichever job they are allocated to.

(c) In a sophisticated system, costs can be analysed both by job (for example all costs related to Job 456), but also by type (for example direct wages incurred on all jobs). It is thus easy to produce control reports and to make comparisons between jobs.

(d) A job costing system might have facilities built into it which incorporate other factors relating to the performance of the job. In complex jobs, sophisticated planning techniques might be employed to ensure that the job is performed in the minimum time possible. Time management features may therefore be incorporated into job costing software.

Cost plus pricing

2.16 At the beginning of this chapter we described the usual method of fixing selling prices within a jobbing concern. It is known as 'cost plus' pricing because a desired profit margin is added to total costs to arrive at the selling price. It has a number of weaknesses.

(a) It offers no incentive to control costs as a profit is guaranteed.

(b) There is no motive to tackle inefficiencies or waste.

(c) It takes no account of the demand for a product (that is, the way in which the selling price affects the demand).

(d) The total cost (and hence the price) is dependent upon the arbitrary nature of the basis of apportionment of overhead costs.

2.17 Despite these weaknesses, the cost plus system is often adopted where one-off jobs are carried out to customers' specifications.

Mark-up and margin

2.18 Consider the following formula.

	%
Cost of sales	100
Plus profit	25
Equals sales	$\underline{125}$

Profit may be expressed either as a percentage of cost of sales (such as 25% (25/100) *mark-up* using the formula above) as in cost plus pricing or as a percentage of sales (such as 20% (25/125) *margin*).

Job costing for internal services

2.19 It is possible to use a job costing system to control the costs of an internal service department, such as the maintenance department or the printing department. If a job costing system is used, the user departments can be charged for the cost of specific jobs carried out for them, rather than apportioning the total costs of these service departments to the user departments using an arbitrarily determined apportionment basis.

3   AN ILLUSTRATION OF JOB COSTING

3.1 An example may help to illustrate the principles of job costing, and the way in which the costing of individual jobs fits in with the recording of total costs in control accounts.

Example: Job costing

3.2 Fothebys Ltd is a jobbing company. On 1 June 19X2, there was one uncompleted job in the factory. The job card for this work is summarised as follows.

Job Cost Card, Job No 6832

Costs to date	£
Direct materials	630
Direct labour	350
Production overhead	240
Production cost to date	$\underline{1,220}$

During June, a new job (job 6833) was started in the factory. Production costs were as follows.

Direct materials	£
Issued to: job 6832	2,390
job 6833	3,700
Damaged stock written off from stores	2,300
Material transfers	
Job 6832 to job 6833	620
Materials returned to stores	
From job 6832	870
Direct labour hours recorded	
Job 6832	430 hrs
Job 6833	280 hrs

The cost of labour hours during June 19X2 was £3 per hour, and production overhead is absorbed at the rate of £2 per direct labour hour. Production overheads incurred during the month amounted to £3,800.

The jobs were delivered to customers as soon as they were completed, and the invoiced amounts were as follows.

		£
Job 6832		5,500
Job 6833		8,000

Administration and marketing overheads are added to the cost of sales at the rate of 20% of production cost. Actual costs incurred during June 19X2 amounted to £3,200.

Prepare the summarised job cost cards for each job, and calculate the profit on each completed job.

Solution: Job costing

3.3 *Job cards, summarised*

	Job 6832	*Job 6833*
	£	£
Materials (W)	1,530	4,320
Labour	1,640	840
Production overhead	1,100	560
Factory cost	4,270	5,720
Admin & marketing o'hd (20%)	854	1,144
Cost of sale	5,124	6,864
Invoice value	5,500	8,000
Profit/(loss) on job	376	1,136

Working

Materials for job 6832: £(630 + 2,390 – 620 – 870) = £1,530
Materials for job 6833: £(3,700 + 620) = £4,320

3.4 We gave you some information in the example to 'distract' you. Damaged stock written off cannot be identified with any particular job and so will form part of the overheads to be spread over all jobs. Similarly actual costs of administration and selling are not relevant because a predetermined percentage is used for costing purposes.

4   BATCH COSTING

What is a batch?

4.1 A batch is a cost unit which consists of a separate, readily identifiable group of product units which maintain their separate identity throughout the production process.

4.2 There is a rather grey area between batch production and continuous processing (which we will be looking at in the next section): the end result of both production methods will be lots of identical items. Each batch is separate and identifiable (like a job) but within a particular batch all the individual items of product are identical, just like the final output from a process.

Batch costing

4.3 Costing when the cost unit is a batch is no different to costing when the cost unit is a job. The documentation may differ in some respects - for example the labour costs may be derived from piecework tickets and time sheets rather than job cards - but it will still allow specific costs to be identified with specific batches.

4.4 The cost per unit is the total batch cost divided by the number of units in the batch.

5 WHAT IS PROCESS COSTING?
Centrally assessed 6/97

5.1 Process costing is used where it is not possible to identify separate units of production, or jobs. Process costing occurs in continuous production such as oil refining, or the manufacture of soap, paint, textiles, paper, foods and drinks, many chemicals and so on. Process costing may also be associated with the continuous production of large volumes of low-cost items, such as cans or tins.

5.2 The important features of process costing systems are:

(a) clearly defined process cost centres and the accumulation of all costs by the cost centre;

(b) the maintenance of accurate records of whole and part units produced and the costs incurred by each process;

(c) the averaging of total costs of every process over the total production of each process, including whole and partly-completed units;

(d) where a series of separate processes is required, the output of one process (finished product of that process) becomes the input (direct material) of the next until the final output (ultimate product) is made in the final process.

5.3 You must appreciate that the procedures and documents used in the recording of cost information when process costing is in use are no different from what we have seen already. Process costing is simply a way of deriving a valuation for output and stock in a processing industry.

5.4 Process costing is designed to deal with the following situations.

(a) The continuous nature of production in many processes means that there will usually be closing work in progress which must be valued. In process costing it is not possible to build up cost records of the cost per unit of output or the cost per unit of closing stock because production in progress is an indistinguishable homogeneous mass.

(b) There is often a loss in progress (or 'in process') due to spoilage, wastage, evaporation and so on.

(c) Output from production may be a single product, but there may also be a by-product (or by-products) and/or joint products.

6 THE AIMS OF PROCESS COSTING

6.1 Suppose that a company operates a two-stage manufacturing process. Details of each process are shown below.

Process 1

Costs incurred	£10,000
Units processed	1,000

Process 2

Units transferred from process 1	1,000
Costs incurred	£20,000
Units completed	1,000

6.2 Process costing aims to do nothing more than spread the cumulative costs incurred over the units processed. So for process 1 we can calculate the cost per unit as follows.

$$\text{Cost per unit} = \frac{\text{costs incurred}}{\text{units processed}} = \frac{£10,000}{1,000} = £10 \text{ per unit}$$

The units are then transferred to process 2 at a cost of £10 each. The total cost of units transferred becomes part of the cumulative costs incurred. For process 2 the cost per unit is calculated as follows.

$$\text{Cost per unit} = \frac{\text{costs incurred}}{\text{units processed}} = \frac{(1,000 \times £10) + £20,000}{1,000} = £30 \text{ per unit}$$

6.3 Let us look at another simple example. Suppose that Purr and Miaow Ltd make squeaky toys for cats. Production of the toys involves two processes, shaping and colouring. During the year to 31 March 19X3, 1,000,000 units of material worth £500,000 were input to the first process, shaping. Direct labour costs of £200,000 and production overhead costs of £200,000 were also incurred in connection with the shaping process. There were no opening or closing stocks in the shaping department. The process account for shaping for the year ended 31 March 19X3 would be drawn up as follows.

PROCESS 1 (SHAPING) ACCOUNT

	Units	£		Units	£
Direct materials	1,000,000	500,000	Output to Process 2	1,000,000	900,000
Direct labour		200,000			
Production overheads		200,000			
	1,000,000	900,000		1,000,000	900,000

The units columns in the process account are added for memorandum purposes only. They help you to ensure that you have included all relevant data in the account.

6.4 All output from shaping was transferred to the second process, colouring, during the year to 31 March 19X3. An additional 500,000 units of material, costing £300,000, were input to the colouring process. Direct labour costs of £150,000 and production overhead costs of £150,000 were also incurred. There were no opening or closing stocks in the colouring department. The process account for colouring for the year ended 31 March 19X3 would be drawn up as follows.

PROCESS 2 (COLOURING) ACCOUNT

	Units	£		Units	£
Materials from process 1	1,000,000	900,000	Output to finished		
Added materials	500,000	300,000	goods	1,500,000	1,500,000
Direct labour		150,000			
Production overhead		150,000			
	1,500,000	1,500,000		1,500,000	1,500,000

6.5 The cost per unit of output to finished goods is calculated as follows.

Output to finished goods = 1,500,000 units at total cost of £1,500,000

$$\text{Cost per unit of output} = £\left(\frac{1,500,000}{1,500,000}\right) = £1.00$$

6.6 Direct labour and production overhead may be treated together as 'conversion cost'.

Added materials, labour and overhead in Process 2 are added gradually throughout the process. Materials from Process 1, in contrast, will often be introduced in full at the start of the second process.

6.7 You should try not to forget that however involved the calculations seem to get, this calculation (of a cost per unit) is your ultimate aim in process costing, because it is this calculation that enables you to place a value on the units produced (output) and on closing stocks.

6.8 The calculations do indeed get quite involved, not because there are difficulties in establishing what the costs are, but because problems can arise in deciding about the number of units the costs are to be spread over.

(a) What goes in is not necessarily what comes out: liquids may evaporate, materials may have to be trimmed or shaped or drilled. Sometimes more materials will be lost in this way than at other times and this has to be accounted for. Sometimes the trimmings or other bits of scrap have a value themselves, and this also has to be accounted for (although not at this level of your studies).

(b) Processing is a continuous operation, but accounting for it requires a 'cut-off' point, so there will inevitably be work that is only partly completed at any time (for example a period end) when a costing exercise has to be carried out. It is reasonable to suppose that partly completed units have not yet cost as much to make as fully completed ones, but how do we decide how 'complete' an item is?

6.9 The next two sections deal in turn with losses and then partly completed output.

7 ACCOUNTING FOR WASTE OR LOSS
Centrally assessed 12/96 and 6/97

7.1 During a production process, a loss may occur due to wastage, spoilage, evaporation, and so on. Loss of this type may be divided into two categories.

(a) Loss *expected* during the normal course of operations, for unavoidable reasons. The average expected loss is known as *normal loss*.

(b) *Unexpected* losses, usually known as *abnormal loss*.

7.2 In the case of normal loss, it is argued that the cost of such losses is an inherent part of the production process. If a piece of metal has to have a hole drilled in it then the metal that used to be in the hole is lost: having a hole is part of the production process. In other words, the cost of normal loss is as much a production cost as, say, the cost of materials or labour. In the same way as these other costs, the cost of normal loss is spread across the expected units of good output, to arrive at a unit cost of production.

7.3 With abnormal loss the case is different. It would be unreasonable to include in the valuation of good units of output the costs arising from poor workmanship, poor materials, or accident. Instead, the costs of abnormal loss should be written off to profit and loss account so that they do not affect the valuation of *expected* units of output.

7.4 An example will make this distinction clearer.

Example: Normal and abnormal loss

7.5 Rubbachi Ltd operates a manufacturing process, and during March 19X3 the following processing took place.

Opening stock	nil	Closing stock	nil
Units introduced	1,000 units	Output	900 units
Costs incurred	£4,500	Loss	100 units

What is the cost of output in the following circumstances?

(a) Expected or normal loss is 10% of input
(b) There is no expected loss, so that the entire loss of 100 units was unexpected

Solution: Normal and abnormal loss

7.6 (a) If loss is expected, and is an unavoidable feature of processing, it is argued by cost accountants that there is no point in charging a cost to the loss. It is more sensible to accept that the loss will occur, and spread the costs of production over the expected units of output. In other words, the cost of normal loss is treated just like any other production cost such as the cost of direct labour.

$$\text{Cost per unit of output} = \frac{\text{costs incurred}}{\text{expected output (90\% of 1,000)}} = \frac{£4,500}{900 \text{ units}} = £5 \text{ per unit}$$

Normal loss is not given any cost, so that the process account would appear as follows.

PROCESS ACCOUNT

	Units	£		Units	£
Costs incurred	1,000	4,500	Normal loss	100	0
			Output units	900	4,500
	1,000	4,500		1,000	4,500

It helps to enter normal loss into the process T account, just to make sure that your memorandum columns for units are the same on the debit and the credit sides of the account.

(b) If loss is unexpected and occurred perhaps as a result of poor workmanship, poor quality materials, poor supervision or damage by accident, it is argued that it would be reasonable to charge a cost to the units of loss. The cost would then be transferred to an 'abnormal loss' account, and eventually written off to the profit and loss account as an item of loss in the period. Units of 'good output' would not be burdened with the cost of the loss, so that the cost per unit remains unaltered.

$$\text{Cost per unit of output} = \frac{\text{costs incurred}}{\text{expected output}} = \frac{£4,500}{1,000 \text{ units}} = £4.50 \text{ per unit}$$

The process account and abnormal loss account would look like this.

PROCESS ACCOUNT

	Units	£		Units	£
Costs incurred	1,000	4,500	Abnormal loss	100	450
			Output units	900	4,050
	1,000	4,500		1,000	4,500

ABNORMAL LOSS ACCOUNT

	Units	£		£
Process account	100	450	Profit and loss account	450

Example: Normal and abnormal loss again

7.7 During a four-week period costs of input to a process were £29,070. Input was 1,000 units, output was 850 units and normal loss is 10%. Calculate the cost of output from the process and the cost of any abnormal loss.

Solution: Normal and abnormal loss again

7.8 $\text{Cost per unit} = \dfrac{\text{costs incurred}}{\text{expected output}} = \dfrac{£29,070}{1,000 \times 90\%} = £32.30 \text{ per unit}$

Cost of output = 850 × £32.30 = £27,455

Cost of abnormal loss = (900 − 850) × £32.30 = £1,615

8 PARTLY COMPLETED OUTPUT

8.1 We have assumed so far that opening and closing stocks of work in process have been nil. We must now look at more realistic examples and consider how to allocate the costs incurred in a period between completed output (finished units) and partly completed closing stock.

8.2 Suppose, for example, that an organisation introduces 5,000 units into a process but only manages to complete 4,000 of them in the month. Closing stock of 1,000 units has only had 60% of its materials added and only 60% of the required labour hours have been spent on the units. Total costs in the month were £29,440.

8.3 The problem in this example is to divide the costs of production (£29,440) between the finished output of 4,000 units and the closing stock of 1,000 units. It is argued, with good reason, that a division of costs in proportion to the number of units of each (4,000:1,000) would not be 'fair' because closing stock has not been completed, and has not yet 'received' its full amount of materials and conversion costs, but only 60% of the full amount. The 1,000 units of closing stock, being only 60% complete, are the equivalent of 600 fully worked units.

Equivalent units

8.4 To apportion costs fairly and proportionately, units of partly finished production must be expressed in terms of the equivalent of completed units. 'Equivalent units' then provide a basis for apportioning costs.

	Total units	Completion	Equivalent units
Fully worked units	4,000	100%	4,000
Closing stock	1,000	60%	600
	5,000		4,600

8.5 Equivalent units are the basis for apportioning costs and so we need a 'cost per equivalent unit' as follows.

Total cost	£29,440
Equivalent units	4,600
Cost per equivalent unit	£6.40

8.6 We can now apportion the costs between finished output and closing stock.

Item	Equivalent units	Cost of equivalent unit	Valuation £
Fully worked units	4,000	£6.40	25,600
Closing stock	600	£6.40	3,840
	4,600		29,440

8.7 The process account would be shown as follows.

PROCESS ACCOUNT

	Units	£		Units	£
Costs incurred	5,000	29,440	Output to next process	4,000	25,600
			Closing stock c/f	1,000	3,840
	5,000	29,440		5,000	29,440

8.8 When preparing a process T account, it helps to enter the units first. The units columns are simply memorandum columns, but they help you to make sure that there are no units unaccounted for (for example, a loss).

9   JOINT PRODUCTS AND BY-PRODUCTS

9.1 We have studied process costing up to the point where we have calculated, say, output of process 3 as 50,000 units costing £400,000. This is all very well so long as the process produces 50,000 identical items, but what do we do if the next stage is to send some of the output through one kind of process and the rest through another, resulting in two different sorts of product? The end results may be of two basic types.

(a) *Joint products* are two or more products which are output from the same processing operation, but which are indistinguishable from each other (because they are the same commonly processed materials) up to their point of separation. Joint products have a substantial sales value (or a substantial sales value after further, separate processing has been carried out to make them ready for sale).

(b) A *by-product* is a product which is similarly produced at the same time and from the same common process as the main product or joint products. The distinguishing feature of a by-product is its relatively low sales value.

9.2 The problem, if joint products or by-products are involved, is to split the common costs of processing between the various end products.

Joint products

9.3 Joint products are not separately identifiable until a certain stage is reached in the processing operations. This stage is the '*split-off point*', sometimes referred to as the *separation point*. Costs incurred prior to this point of separation are common or joint costs, and these need to be apportioned in some manner to each of the joint products. In the following sketched example, there are two different split-off points.

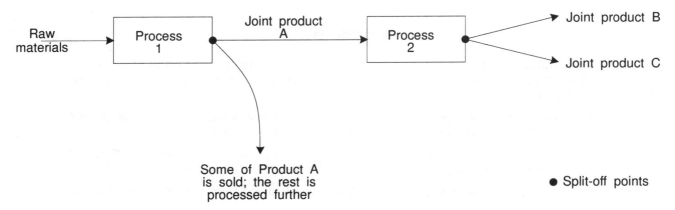

9.4 The problem of costing for joint products concerns joint product costs, those common processing costs shared between the units of eventual output up to their 'split-off point'. Some method needs to be devised for sharing the joint costs between the individual joint products for the following reasons.

(a) To put a value to closing stocks of each joint product.
(b) To record the costs and therefore the profit from each joint product.
(c) Perhaps to assist in pricing decisions.

9.5 Various methods that might be used to establish a basis for apportioning or allocating joint costs to each product are as follows.

(a) *Physical measurement*. For example if two products incur joint costs of £400,000 and the output is 10,000 kg of product 1 and 30,000 kg of product 2, the costs could be split according to the proportions represented by each product to the total output.

Product 1
$$\frac{10,000 \text{kg}}{40,000 \text{kg}} \times £400,000 = £100,000$$

Product 2
$$\frac{30,000 \text{kg}}{40,000 \text{kg}} \times 400,000 = £300,000$$

(b) *Weighted units*. If actual measurement is not appropriate, for example if one product is a gas and another is a liquid, an alternative is to apply some other weighting factor, perhaps derived from a technical analysis that reduces all output to a common basis. Thus product 1 might be given a factor of 3 and product 2 a factor of 7.

Product 1	*Product 2*
$3/10 \times £400,000 = £120,000$	$7/10 \times £400,000 = £280,000$

(c)   According to *sales value at split-off point*. For example if the market value of product 1 at the point where the products separate is £300,000 and that of product 2 is £500,000 the costs could be split 3:5.

Product 1	*Product 2*
$\dfrac{300,000}{800,000} \times £400,000 = £150,000$	$\dfrac{500,000}{800,000} \times £400,000 = £250,000$

(d)   If the products' sales value at split-off point is not known (they may not be saleable in this state) an alternative is to take *the final sales value of each product and deduct the 'post-separation costs'* (which are the costs attributable to each product individually to get them from the point of separation to a state in which they can be sold). For example if product 1 incurs further costs of £50,000 and product 2 £100,000, and the products' final sales values are £300,000 and £500,000 respectively, then the costs will be split $(300,000 - 50,000) : (500,000 - 100,000) = 5:8$.

Product 1	*Product 2*
$5/13 \times £400,000 = £153,846$	$8/13 \times £400,000 = £246,154$

By-products

9.6   A by-product is a supplementary or secondary product (arising as the result of a process) whose value is small relative to that of the principal product. Its accounting treatment usually consists of one of the following.

(a)   Income (minus any post-separation further processing or selling costs) from the sale of the by-product may be added to sales of the main product.

(b)   The sales of the by-product may be treated as a separate, incidental source of income against which are set only post-separation costs (if any) of the by-product.

(c)   The sales income of the by-products may be deducted from the cost of production or cost of sales of the main products.

(d)   The net realisable value of the by-products may be deducted from the cost of production of the main products. The net realisable value is the final saleable value of the by-product minus any post-separation costs. Any closing stock valuation of the main product or joint products would therefore be reduced.

Key topics in this chapter

- Job costing is the costing method used when each cost unit is separately identifiable.

- Batch costing is similar in that each batch of items is separately identifiable.

- Process costing is used where it is not possible to identify separate units of production because of the continuous nature of the production process.

- Process costing is a way of dealing with difficulties that arise in deciding how many units to spread the period's costs over. Difficulties arise because of losses and because some units are only partly finished at any particular point in time.

- Losses may be normal or abnormal.

- The concept of equivalent units is used when units are only partly completed at a particular point in time.

- Processes sometimes give rise to joint products and by-products. If so, further problems arise as to how the common costs of processing should be split between products.

For practice on the points covered in this chapter you should now attempt the Exercises in Session 7 of the Cost Information Workbook

Part D
Standard costing and variance analysis

8 Standard costing

This chapter covers the following topics.

1   Standard costs and standard costing

2   How standards are set

3   Performance standards

4   Responsibility for and revision of standards

---

1 STANDARD COSTS AND STANDARD COSTING
Centrally assessed 6/95

1.1 Do you remember way back in Chapter 2 we mentioned that an easy way of valuing materials issues and materials stock is to use standard costs? Well, you have been rewarded for your patience. In this chapter we will be looking in detail at standard costs including how and why they are set. In the next chapter we will be considering things called variances, which arise as a result of using standard costs, in other words, of using a system of standard costing. Don't worry about these new terms. All will become clearer as you work through this chapter and the next.

What is a standard?

1.2 A *standard* represents what we think should happen. It is our best 'guesstimate' of how long something will take to produce, what quantity of materials it will require, how much it will cost and so on.

1.3 The materials standard for a product is our best estimate of how much material is needed to make the product in kilograms, litres, metres or whatever (standard materials usage) multiplied by our best estimate of the price we will have to pay for each kilogram, litre, metre or whatever (standard materials price). For example, we might think that two square metres of material should be needed to make a skirt and that the material should cost £10 per square metre. The standard material cost of the skirt is therefore 2 × £10 = £20.

1.4 Likewise the labour standard for a product is an estimate of how many hours are needed to make the product multiplied by the amount the labour force needed to make the product is paid per hour.

1.5 The whole idea of a best guesstimate might sound a bit of a hit and miss affair to you. It may seem as if standard setting has no technical basis and that we can make it up as we go along. You would be wrong. As we will explain below, there is a proper approach to setting standards.

What is standard costing?

1.6 Standard costing is the preparation of standard costs for use in the following situations.

(a) In costing as a means of valuing stocks and the cost of production. It is an alternative method of valuation to methods like FIFO, LIFO or replacement costing.

(b) In variance analysis, which is a means of controlling the business.

The standard cost card

1.7 A standard cost card (or standard cost sheet) can be prepared for each product. The card will normally show the quantity and price of each direct material to be consumed, the time and rate of each grade of direct labour required, the overhead recovery and the full cost. The standard selling price and the standard profit per unit may also be shown.

1.8 A distinction should be made in the standard between the following overhead costs.

(a) Fixed and variable production overheads, unless variable overheads are insignificant in value, in which case all production overheads are regarded as fixed costs.

(b) Production overhead and other overheads (administration and marketing). In many costing systems, administration and marketing overheads are excluded from the standard unit cost, so that the standard cost is simply a standard production cost.

1.9   A simple standard cost card might therefore look like the one shown below.

STANDARD COST CARD
PRODUCT ......1234......

DESCRIPTION	QUANTITY	COST PER KG/HOUR/ETC	EXTENSION	TOTAL
Materials			£	£
Flour	3 kg	4.00	12.00	
Water	9 litres	2.00	18.00	
SUB-TOTAL				30.00
Labour				
Duckers	6 hrs	1.50	9.00	
Divers	8 hrs	2.00	16.00	
SUB-TOTAL				25.00
Direct cost				55.00
Variable production o/h	14hrs	0.50		7.00
Standard variable cost				62.00
Fixed production o/h	14hrs	4.50		63.00
Standard full production cost				125.00
Administration o/h				15.00
STANDARD COST OF SALE				140.00
Standard profit				20.00
STANDARD SELLING PRICE				160.00

1.10   In a computer system cost cards could be assembled on a spreadsheet, or by means of a tailor-made programme drawing its information from a database.

2   HOW STANDARDS ARE SET

Establishing standard material costs
Centrally assessed 12/96 and 6/97

2.1   We have already seen that the standard materials cost for a unit of output is calculated as follows:

standard materials usage × standard materials price

To set a standard materials cost we therefore need to establish the standard materials usage and the standard materials price.

Standard usage of materials

2.2 To ascertain how much material should be used to make a product, technical specifications have to be prepared for the product. This will be done by experts in the production department. On the basis of these technical and engineering specifications and in the light of experience, a bill of materials will be drawn up which lists the quantity of materials required to make a unit of the product. These quantities can include allowances for wastage of materials if that is normal and unavoidable.

Standard prices of materials

2.3 The proper approach to setting a standard cost for a particular material is to study the market for that material and become aware of any likely future trends. If your company makes coffee-flavoured ice-cream, news of a disastrous coffee crop failure clearly has implications for raw materials prices and the amounts at which standards should be set.

2.4 In practice it is not always possible or practicable to acquire full information. In such circumstances it is likely that standard prices would be set on the basis of current prices and any notification from suppliers of changes (for example a new catalogue or price list).

2.5 Sometimes businesses are able to enter into a contract stating that such and such a price will be charged for such and such a period. Obviously this adds a good deal of certainty to the standard setting process.

2.6 Standards should also take into account any discount that may be available for bulk purchase, so long as it is economical to buy in sufficiently large quantities to earn the discounts, after considering the costs of holding the stock.

Establishing standard labour costs
Centrally assessed 6/95, 6/96 and 12/96

2.7 In principle it is easy to set standards for labour.

(a) Find out how long it should take to do a job.
(b) Multiply this time by the rate that the person who does the job is paid.

The result is the standard labour cost for that job.

2.8 In practice, of course, it is not this straightforward. For example, an experienced worker may be able to do the job in less time than a novice, and two equally experienced workers may take a different length of time to do the same job. Some time must be spent recording actual performance before a realistic standard can be established.

Example: Labour standards

2.9 A garage employs two mechanics, Will, who is an apprentice, and Jack, who has given loyal service for ten years. The accountant is looking through last week's figures and decides to note down the time each mechanic took to perform each of ten MOTs.

Will	*Jack*
Minutes	Minutes
63	30
55	28
50	35
57	25
49	32
52	33
58	29
57	31
70	30
69	27

Will is presently paid £4.50 per hour and Jack £8 per hour. Calculate the standard time for performing an MOT, the standard labour cost for performing an MOT and the cost of a standard hour.

Solution: Labour standards

2.10 The total time taken for 20 MOTs is 880 minutes, an average of 44 minutes per MOT. Will takes a total of 580 minutes and Jack 300 minutes. Multiplied by their respective hourly rates the total cost is £83.50 or an average of £4.18 per MOT.

Thus, an hour of MOT work costs, on average,

$$\frac{60}{44} \times £4.18 = £5.70$$

We have therefore calculated the following for MOTs.

Standard time	44 minutes
Standard labour cost per MOT	£4.18
Cost of one standard hour	£5.70

2.11 These figures have considerable shortcomings however. They take no account of the time of day when the work was performed, or the type or age of vehicle concerned. We cannot tell to what extent the difference in performance of the two mechanics is due to their relative experience and to what extent it is due to other factors: possibly Will does the more difficult jobs to gain experience, while Jack works on cars that he regularly maintains for established customers who ask for him.

2.12 On the other hand it is quite likely that a better controlled set of measurements would give very similar results to those obtained using historical figures. In a case like this there is probably very little point in trying to be more scientific and 'accurate'. Even if the garage performed 20 MOTs a day, the first set of figures would have to be quite significantly wrong for a more accurate estimation to make any material difference to the accuracy of the costing. (If, however, we were dealing with a high volume business where, say, 10,000 units were produced an hour, then small differences in times and costs per unit (or batch or whatever) would have a considerable impact on the accuracy of the costing. In such cases, the taking of more precise measurements in controlled conditions and the use of sophisticated statistical techniques would be worthwhile.)

2.13 How would these figures affect Will and Jack if they were used as standards? So far as Will is concerned a standard time of 44 minutes is a good target to aim at: he is expected to improve his performance, but he is not expected to be as fast as the more experienced mechanic Jack. For Jack the standard could be demotivating: he may not work so hard if he knows he has half as long again as he needs to do an MOT. A 'time saved bonus' for MOTs taking less than 44 minutes is a good idea in this case: Jack will not slack off if he is financially rewarded for his hard work, and Will has a further incentive to speed up his own work.

Work study and standard costs

2.14 The point about accuracy might be developed here. In the example no special effort was made to record the times taken to perform the MOTs. The standard was calculated using historical data. This approach is widely used in practice. It has two advantages. There is no extra expense in obtaining the information, and it is not distorted by employees who, knowing they are being measured, work more slowly than usual to ensure that easy standards are set.

2.15 The information is, however, distorted by past inefficiencies and 'engineered standards' are therefore considered to be preferable. These are based upon a detailed study of the operations involved in a task. You may have heard of 'time and motion studies', and this is essentially what is involved although the phrase is rather dated. The most commonly used techniques are the following.

(a) *Analytical estimating.* This involves breaking down a job into fairly 'large' units and estimating a time for each unit.

(b) *Predetermined motion time study (PMTS).* This approach uses times established for basic human motions and so the physical motions required to perform the task would first need to be ascertained by observation.

(c) *Synthetic timing.* This technique is used if it is not possible to actually measure how long a job takes, perhaps because the job is still at the drawing board stage.

2.16 The standard times established by such methods are adjusted to allow for any delays that are unavoidable, and also include an allowance for rest, relaxation, calls of nature, fluctuating performance ('off days') and other contingencies such as machine breakdowns.

2.17 You may be wondering why anybody should bother to go to such extreme lengths. Suppose rivets are made in a repetitive operation which is thought to take five seconds per unit produced and operatives are paid a standard £5 per hour. If there are 100 operatives working a seven hour day it is feasible to produce 504,000 ($100 \times 60/5 \times 60 \times 7$) rivets at a cost of £3,500 ($100 \times 7 \times £5$) per day.

If the operation actually takes 6 seconds, not 5, then to produce 504,000 rivets it will really take 840 hours and cost £4,200 or 20% more than expected. Where large volumes and large sums of money are involved it is clearly worth being as accurate as possible.

Standard hour
Centrally assessed 6/97

2.18 Students are sometimes confused by the concept of a *standard hour*. Contrary to what you might expect, a standard hour is not a unit of time. In the example above a standard hour would be 720 rivets, this being the number of rivets that could be produced by one operative in one hour if the operative was working in the *standard way* at the *standard rate*. In the Will/Jack example a standard hour is 1.36 MOTs. In other words a standard hour is a *quantity of work*, not a period of time. You may also come across the term *standard minute:* again this is a quantity of work (12 rivets in our example). A standard hour could be in terms of the output of a machine during one hour rather than labour output.

2.19 The person working in the standard way at the standard rate is said to be working at *standard performance.*

2.20 Other terms, like 'ideal standard' and 'attainable standard' are also of particular relevance to labour costs but we shall come back to these later in the chapter.

Establishing standard costs for expenses

2.21 Cost accounting textbooks are usually silent on the way to set standard costs for expenses, and certainly there is little to add to what you already know about standard setting for materials and labour.

(a) If a contract has been entered into (for cleaning, say) then the standard cost can be set at the amount specified in the contract.

(b) Certain expenses are like materials in that there is a (fluctuating) market rate for a specific quantity and the amount likely to be consumed can be determined by 'engineering' methods (studying the relationship between what is put in and what comes out). Examples are gas and electricity.

2.22 An advantage (for standard setting purposes) with many expenses is that they are fixed over the period for which the standard is being set. The annual buildings insurance premium, for example, will be known for certain on 1 January: it will not turn out to have been different when the year's actual results are determined.

2.23 In other cases expenses can be made to conform to a standard. Discretionary costs, for example, need only be incurred up to a certain level. Suppose you had £10,000 to spend on staff training. Once £10,000 had been spent this would be the end of staff training for the year.

2.24 To conclude we shall show how a standard level of expenditure might be set for energy consumption when it is an overhead cost and how a standard rate per unit might be set for it when it is a direct expense.

Example: Standard costs for expenses

2.25 Pole Pots Ltd uses a number of gas-fired furnaces to make its products. All are connected to a single meter, but all have their own gauges which show how many therms have been consumed. A gas heater in the factory office is also connected to the meter. The gas central heating in the main administrative office is separately metered.

2.26 During the past year one of Pole Pots furnaces produced 2,000 units and used 943 therms. Information from the gas bills for the whole of the period is as follows.

	Administrative office	*Factory*
	£	£
27.1.X1	2,989.48	8,259.37
24.4.X1	2,527.14	6,482.09
29.7.X1	1,398.26	9,961.24
28.10.X1	2,493.82	8,662.55
26.1.X2	3,477.77	8,729.48

Standing charges are £25 per quarter for the administrative office and £50 per quarter for the factory. The price per therm throughout 19X1 was £0.442, but it rose by 10% in January 19X2.

Calculate the total expected cost of gas for the administrative office for 19X2 and the expected cost of gas per unit of production for the individual furnace referred to.

Note. Assume that activity will continue at the same level in 19X2 as in 19X1.

Solution: Standard costs for expenses

2.27 (a) For the administrative office it is reasonable to suppose that gas usage on a daily basis does not vary much although obviously it varies according to the season. We can therefore calculate an annual amount by using the accruals principle.

	£
1.1.X1 to 27.1.X1 (27/91 × (2,989.48 − 25.00))	879.57
28.1.X1 to 24.4.X1 (2,527.14 − 25.00)	2,502.14
25.4.X1 to 29.7.X1 (1,398.26 − 25.00)	1,373.26
30.7.X1 to 28.10.X1 (2,493.82 − 25.00)	2,468.82
29.10.X1 to 31.12.X1 (64/91 × (3,477.77 − 25.00))	2,428.32
	9,652.11
Add 10%	965.21
	10,617.32
Add standing charge (4 × £25)	100.00
Total expected cost	10,717.32

(b) The furnace referred to used 0.4715 therms for each unit of production in 19X1 (943 ÷ 2,000). In 19X2, therefore, the cost per unit of production will be as follows.

$$0.4715 \text{ therms} \times (0.442 \times 1.1) = £0.229 \text{ per unit}$$

2.28 Note that we could now estimate the cost of gas if planned activity was to double the production from this furnace: 4,000 units would cost £916 in direct fuel expenses.

3 PERFORMANCE STANDARDS

3.1 Do not forget that standards are averages. Even under ideal working conditions, it would be unrealistic to expect every unit of activity or production to take exactly the same time, using exactly the same amount of materials, and at exactly the same cost. Some variations are inevitable, but for a reasonably large volume of activity, it would be fair to expect that on average, standard results should be achieved.

3.2 Standard costs are thus 'standard' not only in the sense 'this product has been produced in a standard way, using the standard amount of materials and so on' but also in the sense 'this product has been produced to a certain standard'. There are four different performance standards that an organisation could aim for.

(a) *Ideal standards:* these are based on the most favourable operating conditions, with no wastage, no inefficiencies, no idle time and no breakdowns. Variances from ideal standards are useful for pinpointing areas where a close examination may result in large savings, but they are likely to have an unfavourable motivational impact. Employees will often feel that the goals are unattainable and not work so hard.

(b) *Attainable standards:* these are based on efficient (but not perfect) operating conditions. Some allowance is made for wastage, inefficiencies, machine breakdowns and fatigue. If well-set they provide a useful psychological incentive, and for this reason they should be introduced whenever possible. The consent and co-operation of employees involved in improving the standard are required.

(c) *Current standards:* these are standards based on current working conditions (current wastage, current inefficiencies). The disadvantage of current standards is that they do not attempt to improve on current levels of efficiency, which may be poor and capable of significant improvement.

(d) *Basic standards:* these are standards which are kept unaltered over a long period of time, and may be out-of-date. They are used to show changes in efficiency or performance over an extended time period. Basic standards are perhaps the least useful and least common type of standard in use.

4 RESPONSIBILITY FOR AND REVISION OF STANDARDS

Responsibility for standards

4.1 The responsibility for setting standards should be shared between managers able to provide the necessary levels of expected efficiency, prices and overhead costs.

Revision of standards

4.2 When there is a sudden change in economic circumstances, or in technology or production methods, the standard cost will no longer be accurate. In practice, changing standards frequently is an expensive operation and can cause confusion. For this reason standard cost revisions are usually only made once a year. From the point of view of providing a target, however, an out-of-date standard is useless and some revision may be necessary.

4.3 At times of rapid price inflation, many managers have felt forced to change price and wage rate standards continually. This, however, leads to a reduction in the value of the standard as a yardstick. At the other extreme is the adoption of 'basic' standards which will remain unchanged for many years. They provide a constant base for comparison, but this is hardly satisfactory when, for example, there is technological change in working procedures and conditions.

Standard costing in times of inflation

4.4 Standard costs are usually based on one of the following.

(a) Expected average price levels for the period in question (normally one year)
(b) Current price levels

In the absence of inflation there should be no difference between these two figures.

4.5 Problems arise when there is price or wage rate inflation. If expected average price levels are used as the standard basis, the standard cost will be set at the estimated mid-year price level. In a period of inflation actual prices at the start of the year will be below standard prices and this will have a favourable effect on price variances in the first few periods of the year. By the second half of the year this position will probably have reversed. Problems in interpretation (and therefore control) will thus arise because it is less clear to what extent the favourable or adverse variances reflect changes in performance.

4.6 If the standard cost is based on current price levels the effect of inflation will be to create ever-increasing and unrealistic adverse price variances, possibly disguising the effect of other, controllable trends.

4.7 Standard costing is therefore more difficult in times of inflation but it is still worthwhile.

(a) Usage and efficiency variances will still be meaningful.

(b) Inflation is measurable: there is no reason why its effects cannot be removed from the variances reported.

(c) Standard costs can be revised, so long as this is not done too frequently.

Key points in this chapter

- A standard represents what we think should happen.

- A standard cost is a predetermined unit of cost.

- Standard costing is a means of valuing stocks and the issue of materials to production and a way of exerting control over a business.

- A standard cost card/sheet shows full details of the components making up the standard cost of a product.

- Setting materials standards involves determining how much material is needed to produce a product and how much that material should cost.

- Setting labour standards is generally a matter of estimating how long it will take to do a piece of work. This can be done on a rough and ready basis or by detailed work study.

- Standard costs can be set for expenses just as they can for any other cost.

- Standards are basically set by developing an awareness of market conditions and by understanding technical requirements. They can also be set so as to encourage improvements in performance.

- Remember to consider the effects of inflation when setting standards.

For practice on the points covered in this chapter you should now attempt the Exercises in Session 8 of the Cost Information Workbook

9 Variance analysis

This chapter covers the following topics.

1   What use are standards?

2   Materials variances

3   Labour variances

4   Variable overhead variances

5   Fixed overhead variances

6   Variance reports

7   Investigating variances

8   Cost accounting entries for variances

---

1   WHAT USE ARE STANDARDS?

1.1   Having set standards (as described in the previous chapter), what are we going to do with them? We mentioned that we could use materials standards to value materials issues and materials stock. But what about labour standards? And standards for expenses? As we said earlier, the principal reason most organisations use standard costs is for control.

1.2   Standards represent what should happen. Let's take materials as an example. Suppose 10,000 units of product X should require 10,000 kgs of material A costing £10,000. By comparing what actually happens - 11,000 kgs of material A costing £12,000 were required to make 10,000 units of product X - with what should happen, we can see if we are doing as well as we should be. We are obviously not doing as well as we should be with product X because we had to spend £2,000 more than anticipated and use an extra 1,000 kgs. We can therefore investigate these differences between what should happen and what did happen (the differences are called *variances*) in order to ascertain what went wrong: why the material cost £1.09 per kilogram instead of £1 per kilogram and why 1,000 extra kilograms were needed - and to try to get operations back on course.

2   MATERIALS VARIANCES
Centrally assessed 6/95, 12/95 and 6/97

Why materials variances arise

2.1   Standards are estimates. Their accuracy as predictions of what will happen depends on what happens after they have been set. For example, suppose you are expecting a good coffee bean harvest and have set a standard material price of £10 per kilogram of coffee beans. A good harvest will result in your standard being accurate but a poor harvest, leading to prices of £15 per kilogram of coffee beans, results in an inaccurate standard. Or suppose your recipe for coffee flavoured ice-creams requires 1 kg of coffee beans to make 10 litres of ice cream. Government regulations introduced six months after the standard was set stipulating 1.5 kg of coffee beans to make 10 litres of ice cream would mean that what actually happens is not what is expected.

2.2   Bear in mind, also, that standard costs are average costs. The manner in which they are set means that they are costs that you can expect to achieve, on average, over a reasonably large volume of production. Even under ideal working conditions controlled by computers it is unlikely that every unit will use exactly the same amount of materials at exactly the same cost.

2.3   Because standards are estimates and averages it is more than likely that there will be differences (variances) between the standard materials cost and the cost actually incurred.

2.4   Think back to how the materials standard cost is calculated: standard usage × standard price. Now think about how a variance could arise.

(a)   If actual usage were different to standard usage there would be a variance.

(b)   If standard price were different to actual price there would be a variance.

(c)   If standard usage and standard price were different to actual usage and actual price there would be a variance.

Calculating materials variances

2.5   There are a number of different approaches to calculating variances. We shall describe two.

2.6   The best approach we shall call the 'what happened' approach. This is the best approach because it means that you understand why the difference occurred. If you do not learn to think in these terms straightaway, variance analysis will become nothing more than a mechanical process of plugging numbers into formulae rather than an extremely useful cost accounting technique.

Example: The 'what happened' approach

2.7 The standards that have been set for materials cost and usage for a product, together with actual production figures for the first month of production are shown below. Your task is to work out what happened and calculate variances as appropriate.

	Standard cost	*Standard usage*
Material A	£2.20 per kg	2kg per unit

Actual production in month 1	10,000 units
Actual cost of material A	£46,000

Usage in month 1 was exactly as expected.

Solution: The 'what happened' approach

2.8 10,000 units should have taken 20,000kg of material A and we know that this is what happened because we are told. So far as usage is concerned, then, there are no differences, and no variances to calculate.

2.9 Material A should have cost 20,000kg × £2.20, or £44,000, if standard prices had been paid, but material A actually cost £46,000. It is easy enough to see that what happened is that the price actually paid per kg for material A must have been £2.30 per kg. This is 10p per kg, or 20p per unit, more than expected. The total difference in cost is 10,000 units × 20p or £2,000.

Example: Further complications

2.10 In month 2 the standards stayed the same but actual production figures were as follows.

Actual production	10,000 units
Material A	21,000 kg costing £47,250

Again your task is to work out what happened and calculate variances as appropriate.

Solution: Further complications

2.11 Material A seems to have been used in larger quantities than expected and at a different price.

Instead of costing £44,000, 10,000 units have cost £47,250.

2.12 What has happened in unit terms is as follows.

The cost of material A was $\dfrac{£47,250}{21,000 \text{ kg}} = £2.25$ per kg

The usage of material A was $\dfrac{21,000 \text{ kg}}{10,000 \text{ units}} = 2.1$ kg per unit

2.13 The difference in *price* is the responsibility of the buying department. They paid £2.25 per kg instead of £2.20 per kg and so the part of the total difference attributable to them is 21,000 kg × 5p = £1,050.

2.14 The difference in *usage* is the responsibility of the production department. They used 1,000 kg too many, but it is not their fault that a higher price than standard was paid so it is not fair to attribute the extra 5p to them. Their part of the total difference is therefore valued at standard cost: 1,000 kg × £2.20 = £2,200.

2.15 Adding these variances together shows how the total difference can be broken down.

	£
Price variance	1,050
Usage variance	2,200
Total variance	3,250

Initial summary

2.16 Two variances may therefore be calculated for materials.

(a) The *materials price variance* measures the difference between the actual amount of money paid and the amount of money that should have been paid for the actual quantity of materials.

(b) The *materials usage variance* measures the difference between the actual physical quantity of materials used and the quantity that should have been used for the actual volume of production. (Don't forget this variance is valued at standard cost.)

Example: The 'line by line' method

2.17 The line by line method of calculating variances is not really different from the what happened method, it is just a convenient way of laying out your statement of what happened. Thus for month 2 in the above example, the 'line by line' approach is as follows.

	£
21,000 kg should have cost (× £2.20)	46,200
but did cost	47,250
Materials price variance	1,050

10,000 units should have taken (× 2 kg)	20,000 kg
but did take	21,000 kg
Usage variance in kg	1,000 kg
× standard cost per kg	× £2.20
Materials usage variance	£2,200

Adverse and favourable variances

2.18 All of the examples we have seen so far have been cases where more money was paid out or more materials were used than expected. These are called *adverse variances* because they have adverse consequences. They mean that *less profit* is made than we hoped.

2.19 Sometimes, of course, things will be cheaper than usual or we will use them more efficiently. When less money is paid than expected or fewer materials are used than expected the variances are said to be *favourable variances*. They mean that *more profit* is made than we hoped.

Example: Adverse and favourable variances

2.20 It is now month 4 and actual data is as follows.

Production	9,500 units
Material A	20,000 kg costing £42,000

Have a go at calculating the variances yourself before looking at the solution.

Solution: Adverse and favourable variances

2.21 Let's begin by calculating the materials total variance.

	£
9,500 units should have cost (9,500 × 2kg × £2.20)	41,800
but did cost	42,000
	200 (A)

The (A) indicates that overall the variance is adverse.

2.22 We can now go on to calculate the individual components of the total variance.

	£
20,000 kg should cost (× £2.20)	44,000
but did cost	42,000
Materials price variance	2,000 (F)

The (F) indicates that this is a *favourable* variance because less money was spent than expected.

9,500 units should take (× 2 kg)	19,000 kg
but did take	20,000 kg
Usage variance in kg	1,000 kg (A)
× standard cost per kg	× £2.20
Usage variance in £	£2,200 (A)

The (A) indicates that this is an *adverse* variance, because more materials were used than standard for 9,500 units.

2.23 Let's check that the total variance is the sum of the two individual variances.

	£
Price variance	2,000 (F)
Usage variance	(2,200) (A)
Total variance	(200) (A)

Remember that adverse variances are negative (*less* profit) and favourable variances are positive (*more* profit).

Materials variances and opening and closing stock

2.24 Suppose that a company uses raw material P in production, and that this raw material has a standard price of £3 per metre. During one month 6,000 metres are bought for £18,600, and 5,000 metres are used in production. At the end of the month, stock will have been increased by 1,000 metres.

2.25 Assume that we want to calculate the material price variance. We have a problem. Should it be calculated on the basis of materials *purchased* (6,000 metres) or on the basis of materials *used* (5,000 metres)?

2.26 The answer to this problem depends on how closing stocks of the raw materials are valued.

   (a) If they are valued at *standard cost* (1,000 units at £3 per unit) the price variance is calculated on material *purchases* in the period.

   (b) If they are valued at *actual cost* (using FIFO, 1,000 units at £3.10 per unit), the price variance is calculated on materials *used* in production in the period.

2.27 A full standard costing system is more often than not in operation and so the price variance is calculated on purchases in the period. The variance on the full 6,000 metres will be written off to the costing profit and loss account in the current period, even though only 5,000 metres are included in the cost of production.

Reasons for variances
Centrally assessed 12/95 and 6/97

2.28   As well as calculating the variances, it is important to understand why they might arise.

2.29   Possible reasons for a *materials price variance* may include:

(a)   purchase of a cheaper (favourable) or more expensive (adverse) substitute, than anticipated when the standard cost was set

(b)   bulk buying leading to unforeseen discount (favourable)

(c)   more care taken in purchasing materials (favourable) or less care (adverse)

(d)   material price increase (adverse) or decrease (favourable)

2.30   Possible reasons for a *materials usage variance* may include:

(a)   defective material (adverse) or material used of a higher quality than standard (favourable)

(b)   material used more efficiently (favourable) or excessive waste (adverse)

(c)   theft (adverse)

(d)   stricter quality control (adverse)

Interdependence between variances

2.31   An important additional consideration is that variances should not be seen in isolation. In the example in Paragraphs 2.18 - 2.23 above, the production manager was asked to explain why he had used 1,000 units more than he should have done. He said that the latest batch of material A had been rather poor quality and a lot of it had had to be thrown away. On further investigation it transpired that the buying department had indeed bought a lower grade of material, retailing at £2.10 per kg rather than the standard £2.20. This shows how important it is to understand the real reason for variances. The actions of one part of a business affect the outcome of other parts.

3   LABOUR VARIANCES
Centrally assessed 6/95 and 6/96

3.1   Labour variances are very similar to materials variances but they have different names, presumably because it is thought rather undignified to talk about 'usage' of people and the 'price' of people.

3.2   For labour the money variance is called the *rate variance* and the quantity variance is called the *efficiency variance*.

3.3   Apart from the different names there is no difference between a labour variance and a materials variance.

3.4   The *labour rate variance* is the difference between the actual amount of money paid to labour and the amount that should have been paid for the actual number of hours of work. An adverse rate variance might arise because of a wage rate increase whereas a favourable rate variance could occur if a worker (such as an apprentice) was used with a rate of pay lower than standard.

3.5   The *labour efficiency variance* is the difference between the number of hours actually taken and the number that should have been taken for the actual volume of production, valued at the standard rate per hour.

3.6 An adverse efficiency variance arises if lost time is in excess of that allowed by the standard, if output is lower than the standard or because of deliberate restriction, lack of training or the use of sub-standard material. A favourable efficiency variance arises if output is produced more quickly than expected because of motivation or better quality equipment or materials.

3.7 The 'line by line' method and the 'what happened' method of calculating variances are very similar and, as both were covered earlier in the chapter, we will only consider the line by line method here.

Example: Labour variances

3.8 Suppose that the labour standard for the production of a unit of product B is as follows.

4 hours of grade S labour at £3 per hour

During May 19X0 200 units of product B were made and the direct labour cost of grade S labour was £2,440 for 785 hours work.

See if you can calculate the direct labour total variance, the direct labour rate variance and the direct labour efficiency variance before looking at our solution. The approach is exactly the same as that used for the calculation of material variances.

Solution: Labour variances

3.9 Let us begin by calculating the direct labour total variance.

	£
200 units of product B should have cost (× £12)	2,400
but did cost	2,440
Direct labour total variance	40 (A)

3.10 Having learned that direct labour costs were £40 more than they should have been, we can now look at why this happened.

3.11 *Labour rate variance.* This variance is calculated by taking the number of labour hours 'purchased' ie paid for, and comparing what they did cost with what they should have cost.

	£
785 hours of grade S labour should cost (× £3)	2,355
but did cost	2,440
Labour rate variance	85 (A)

The variance is adverse because actual rates of pay were higher than expected.

3.12 *Labour efficiency variance.* This variance is calculated by taking the amount of output produced (200 units of product B) and comparing how long it should have taken to make them with how long it did take. The difference is the efficiency variance, expressed in hours of work. It should be converted into £ by applying the standard rate per labour hour.

200 units of product B should take (× 4 hours)	800 hrs
but did take	785 hrs
Labour efficiency variance in hrs	15 hrs (F)
× standard rate per hour	× £3
Labour efficiency variance in £	£45 (F)

The variance is favourable because the labour force has been more efficient than expected.

3.13 *Summary*

	£
Labour rate variance	85 (A)
Labour efficiency variance	45 (F)
Direct labour total variance	40 (A)

3.14 Let us continue with the same example. Suppose that during June 19X0 200 units of product B were again made at a direct labour cost of £2,370. The direct labour were paid for 790 hours but were actually idle for 10 hours because of machine breakdowns. See if you can calculate the variances before reading on.

3.15 Let us start, as usual, by calculating the labour total variance.

	£
200 units should have cost (× £12)	2,400
but did cost	2,370
Labour total variance	30 (F)

3.16 Try and calculate a rate variance.

	£
790 hours should cost (× £3)	2,370
but did cost	2,370
Labour rate variance	-

3.17 There is no labour rate variance but the total variance of £30 is not just an efficiency variance because there is a difference between the hours worked and the hours paid for it.

This variance is usually called the *idle time variance*. The easiest way of calculating is simply to multiply the number of hours of idle time by the standard rate per hour.

10 hours × £3 = £30 (A)

3.18 The efficiency variance is calculated as normal.

200 units should take (× 4 hours)	800 hrs
but did take	780 hrs
Labour efficiency variance in hrs	20 hrs (F)
× standard rate per hour	× £3
Labour efficiency variance	£60 (F)

3.19 The total variance, despite the idle time of ten hours, is £30 favourable since the labour force were extra productive in the hours they did work.

Example: All the variances

3.20 In case you are a little confused about how idle time variances fit in the overall scheme, a final example should make it clear.

Continuing with the previous example, in July 19X0 200 units of product B were made as usual. The grade S labour were paid £2,624 for 820 hours although during the month a bottleneck in the production process meant that 30 hours were recorded as idle time. Calculate variances to explain why the production of the 200 units did not cost the standard amount.

Solution: All the variances

3.21 We start by calculating a labour total variance.

	£
200 units should have cost	2,400
but did cost	2,624
Labour total variance	224 (A)

3.22 Now let us look at the rate variance

	£
820 hours should have cost (× £3)	2,460
but did cost	2,624
Labour rate variance	164 (A)

3.23 The idle time, the difference between hours paid and hours worked, gives rise to a variance.

Hours paid for	820 hrs
Hours worked	790 hrs
Idle time	30 hrs (A)
× standard rate per hour	× £3
Idle time variance	£90 (A)

3.24 The efficiency variance is calculated as follows.

200 units should take (× 4 hours)	800 hrs
but did take	790 hrs
Labour efficiency variance (hrs)	10 hrs (F)
× standard rate per hour	× £3
Labour efficiency variance	£30 (F)

Reasons for variances
Centrally assessed 12/96

3.25 Reasons for labour rate variances may include:

(a) wage rate increases (adverse);

(b) using more skilled (and hence more expensive) labour (adverse) or less skilled (and hence less expensive) labour (favourable) than allowed for when the standard was set.

3.26 Favourable labour efficiency variances will be reflected in output being produced more quickly than expected. Reasons may include:

(a) highly motivated or skilled staff;
(b) better quality equipment or materials than anticipated when the standard was set.

3.27 By contrast adverse labour efficiency variances will be reflected in output being lower than the standard set. Reasons may include:

(a) deliberate go-slows;
(b) untrained or unskilled workforce;
(c) substandard material being used.

Interdependence between variances
Centrally assessed 12/96

3.28 Do not forget that variances should not be looked at in isolation. There may be a favourable labour rate variance if apprentices are used instead of the expected skilled labour but this could lead to an adverse efficiency variance if the apprentices do not work as efficiently. On the other hand, more highly skilled workers may be more efficient but their rate per hour will be more. Moreover, if the purchasing department purchases cheaper materials than standard there will be a favourable material price variance but there may be an adverse labour efficiency variance: cheaper material is often of a poorer quality and hence the labour force may take longer to produce a certain quantity of 'good' units.

Efficiency, capacity and production volume ratios
Centrally assessed 12/96

3.29 You may also meet labour activity being measured by ratios, for example:
    (a) Efficiency ratio (or productivity ratio)
    (b) Capacity ratio
    (c) Production volume ratio, or activity ratio (the product of efficiency and capacity ratios).

Efficiency ratio	*Capacity ratio*	*Production volume ratio*
$\dfrac{\text{Standard hours to make actual output}}{\text{Actual hours worked}} \times$	$\dfrac{\text{Actual hours worked}}{\text{Hours budgeted}} =$	$\dfrac{\text{Output measured in expected or standard hours}}{\text{Hours budgeted}}$

These ratios are usually expressed as percentages.

Example: ratios

3.30 Rush and Fluster Ltd budgets to make 25,000 standard units of output (in four hours each) during a budget period of 100,000 hours.

Actual output during the period was 27,000 units which took 120,000 hours to make.

Required

Calculate the efficiency, capacity and production volume ratios.

Solution

3.31 (a) Efficiency ratio $\dfrac{(27,000 \times 4) \text{ hours}}{120,000 \text{ hours}}$ $\times 100\% =$ 90%

    (b) Capacity ratio $\dfrac{120,000 \text{ hours}}{100,000 \text{ hours}}$ $\times 100\% =$ 120%

    (c) Production volume ratio $\dfrac{(27,000 \times 4) \text{ hours}}{100,000 \text{ hours}}$ $\times 100\% =$ 108%

    (d) The production volume ratio of 108% (more output than budgeted) is explained by the 120% capacity working, offset to a certain extent by the poor efficiency (90% × 120% = 108%).

4   VARIABLE OVERHEAD VARIANCES

4.1 Suppose that variable overhead is incurred on a time basis at £1.50 per hour. Product D takes 2 hours to make and so its variable overhead will be 2 hours at £1.50 = £3 per unit.

During July 19X3, 400 units of product D were made. The labour force worked 820 hours, of which 60 hours were recorded as idle time. The actual variable overhead cost was £1,230. Calculate the variable overhead total variance.

4.2

	£
400 units of product D should cost, in variable overhead (× £3)	1,200
but did cost	1,230
Variable overhead total variance	30 (A)

4.3   You would not normally be asked at this level about the constituent variances of the variable overhead total variance. However, for reference, and just in case you encounter these variances unexpectedly early, we will discuss the two variances that combine to give the variable overhead total variance.

4.4   The *variable overhead expenditure variance* arises from the hourly rate of spending on variable production overheads being higher or lower than it should have been.

4.5   The *variable overhead efficiency variance* arises from the labour force working less or more efficiently, and taking longer or shorter to make the output than it should have done. This means that spending on variable overhead was higher or lower than it should have been. The variable overhead efficiency variance is exactly the same, in hours, as the direct labour efficiency variance.

4.6   It is usually assumed that variable overheads are incurred during active working hours, but are not incurred during idle time (for example the machines are not running, therefore power is not being consumed, and no direct materials are being used). This means in our example that although the labour force was paid for 820 hours, they were actively working for only 760 of those hours and so variable production overhead spending occurred during 760 hours.

Example : Variable overhead variances

4.7   Suppose the variable overhead is absorbed at a rate of £5 per labour hour. The labour standard for production of product C was 4 hours.

During June 500 units of product C were made. Variable overheads incurred were £10,690, and total labour hours for June were 1,920 hours. There was no idle time. Try and calculate the variable overhead total variance, the variable overhead expenditure variance and the variable overhead efficiency variance. Remember that the approach is the same as the approach to calculating labour variances.

Solution : Variable overhead variances

4.8   Let us start by calculating the variable overhead total variance

	£
500 units of product C should have cost (x £5 x 4)	10,000
but did cost	10,690
Variable overhead total variance	690 (A)

We can see variable overheads were £690 more than budgeted; let us check why.

4.9   *Variable overhead expenditure variance.* This variance is calculated by taking the number of labour hours actually worked and comparing the amount of variable overhead that should have been incurred in the *actual* hours actively worked, and the actual amount of variable overhead incurred.

	£
1,920 hours of variable overhead should cost (×£5)	9,600
but did cost	10,690
Variable overhead expenditure variance	1,090 (A)

4.10 *Variable overhead efficiency variance*. If you already know the direct labour efficiency variance, the variable overhead efficiency variance is exactly the same in hours, but priced at the variable overhead rate per hour. In our example, the efficiency variance would be as follows:

500 units of product C should take (x 4 hrs)	2,000 hrs
but did take (active hrs)	1,920 hrs
Variable overhead efficiency variance in hrs	80 hrs (F)
x standard rate per hour	× £5
Variable overhead efficiency variance	£400 (F)

4.11 *Summary*

	£
Variable overhead expenditure variance	1,090 (A)
Variable overhead efficiency variance	400 (F)
Variable overhead total variance	690 (A)

4.12 Reasons for variable overhead variances may include:

(a) increases (adverse) or decreases (favourable) in costs incurred;
(b) more economical use of services (favourable).

5 FIXED OVERHEAD VARIANCES

5.1 You should have noticed that the method of calculating labour and materials variances is essentially the same. Fixed overhead variances are, however, somewhat different. When absorption costing is being used they are an attempt to explain the under or over absorption of fixed overheads. You should, of course, know all about under/over absorption of fixed overheads. We looked at it in detail in Chapter 5. If you need reminding, however, skim through Section 6 of that chapter again. Once again you would not normally be assessed on the constituent fixed overhead variances but we briefly discuss them here as a means of demonstrating why the total fixed overhead variance arises.

5.2 You will find it easier to calculate and understand fixed overhead variances if you keep in mind the whole time the fact that you are trying to 'explain' (put a name and value to) any under- or over-absorbed overhead. Remember that the absorption rate is calculated as follows:

$$\text{Overhead absorption rate} = \frac{\text{budgeted fixed overhead}}{\text{budgeted activity level}}$$

5.3 If either the number on top (numerator) or the number on the bottom (denominator) or both are incorrect then we will have under- or over-absorbed overhead.

(a) The *fixed overhead price variance* (also referred to as the *fixed overhead expenditure variance*)occurs if the numerator is incorrect. It measures the under- or over-absorbed overhead caused by the actual total overhead expenditure being different from budget.

Therefore, price variance = budgeted expenditure – actual expenditure

(b)   The *fixed overhead usage and capacity variances* occur if the denominator is incorrect. They measure the under- or over-absorbed overhead caused by the actual activity level being different from the budgeted activity level used in calculating the absorption rate. They therefore show the benefit of working above (or the cost of working below) the budgeted activity level.

5.4   There are two reasons why the actual activity level may be different from the budgeted activity level used in calculating the absorption rate.

(a)   The workforce may have worked more or less efficiently than standard. This is measured by the *fixed overhead usage variance*. (In some systems this may be referred to as the *fixed overhead efficiency variance*).

(b)   Regardless of the level of efficiency of the workforce, the hours worked could have been different to the budgeted hours (because of overtime, strikes and so on). This is measured by the *fixed overhead capacity variance*.

Usage variance =   (number of hours that *actual* production *should* have taken – number of hours *actually* taken) × standard absorption rate per hour

Capacity variance =   (budgeted hours of work – actual hours of work) × standard absorption rate per hour

The combination of these two variances is sometimes referred to as the *fixed overhead volume variance*.

5.5   Let's look at an example. It might help to make a tricky topic a bit clearer.

Example: Price, usage and capacity variances

5.6   A company budgets to produce 1,000 units of product E during August 19X3. The expected time to produce a unit of E is five hours and the budgeted fixed overhead is £20,000. The absorption rate per hour is therefore £20,000/(1,000 × 5) = £4 and the standard fixed overhead cost per unit of product E is 5 hours at £4 per hour, £20 per unit. Actual fixed overhead expenditure in August 19X3 turns out to be £20,450. The labour force manage to produce 1,100 units of product E in 5,400 hours of work. Calculate the appropriate overhead variances.

Solution: Price, usage and capacity variances

5.7   (a)

	£
Fixed overhead incurred	20,450
Fixed overhead absorbed (1,100 × £20)	22,000
Total fixed overhead variance (= over-absorbed overhead)	1,550 (F)

The variance is favourable because overhead has been over absorbed.

(b)

	£
Budgeted fixed overhead expenditure	20,000
Actual fixed overhead expenditure	20,450
Fixed overhead price variance	450 (A)

(c)

Actual production should have taken (1,100 × 5 hrs)	5,500 hrs
but did take	5,400 hrs
Usage variance in hrs	100 hrs (F)
× standard rate per hour	× £4
Usage variance in £	£400 (F)

(d)

	Budgeted hours of work	5,000 hrs
	Actual hours of work	5,400 hrs
	Capacity variance in hours	400 hrs (F)
	× standard absorption rate per hour	× £4
	Capacity variance in £	£1,600 (F)

The variance is favourable because the labour force worked longer than budgeted and so, in theory, output should be *greater* than budgeted.

(e) *Summary*

	£
Price variance	450 (A)
Usage variance	400 (F)
Capacity variance	1,600 (F)
Over-absorbed overhead	1,550 (F)

Reasons for fixed overhead variances

5.8 A *fixed overhead usage variance* could occur because of services being used more economically (favourable).

5.9 A *fixed overhead capacity variance* occurs because actual activity level differs from budgeted activity level. This may be due to poor production scheduling, leading to bottlenecks and low output, unexpected machine breakdowns, strikes or shortage of labour or materials, acts of God (such as floods) and so on.

6 VARIANCE REPORTS

6.1 So far, we have considered how different types of variances are calculated without considering how they may be reported to management.

6.2 An extensive example will now be introduced, both to revise the variance calculations already described, and to consider how they could be reported.

Example: Variances and reports

6.3 Altogether Ltd manufactures one product, and the entire product is sold as soon as it is produced. There are no opening or closing stocks and work in progress is negligible. The company operates a standard costing system and analysis of variances is made every month. The standard cost card for the product, a 'combo', is as follows.

COMBO

		£
Direct materials	0.5 kilos at £4 per kilo	2.00
Direct wages	2 hours at £2.00 per hour	4.00
Variable overheads	2 hours at £0.30 per hour	0.60
Fixed overhead	2 hours at £3.70 per hour	7.40
Standard cost		14.00

Budgeted output for the month of June 19X7 was 5,100 units. Actual results for June 19X7 were as follows.

Production was 4,850 units.
Materials consumed in production amounted to 2,300 kilos at a total cost of £9,800.
Labour hours paid for amounted to 8,500 hours at a cost of £16,800.
Actual operating hours amounted to 8,000 hours.
Variable overheads amounted to £2,600.
Fixed overheads amounted to £42,300.

Calculate all cost variances.

Solution: Variances and reports

6.4   (a)

		£
2,300 kg of material should cost (× £4)		9,200
but did cost		9,800
Materials price variance		600 (A)

(b)

4,850 combos should use (× 0.5kg)	2,425 kgs
but did use	2,300 kgs
Materials usage variance in kgs	125 kgs (F)
× standard cost per kg	× £4
Materials usage variance	£500 (F)

(c)

	£
8,500 hours of labour should cost (× £2)	17,000
but did cost	16,800
Labour rate variance	200 (F)

(d)

To make 4,850 combos should take (× 2hrs)	9,700 hrs
but did take (active hours)	8,000 hrs
Labour efficiency variance in hrs	1,700 hrs (F)
× standard cost per hour	× £2
Labour efficiency variance	£3,400 (F)

(e)   Idle time variance: 500 hours (A) × £2   £1,000 (A)

(f)

	£
8,000 hours should cost (× £0.30)	2,400
but did cost	2,600
Variable overhead expenditure variance	200 (A)

(g)

	£
To make 4,850 combos should take (× 2 hrs)	9,700
but did take	8,000
Variable overhead efficiency variance in hrs	1,700 hrs (F)
× standard cost per hour	£0.30
Variable overhead efficiency variance	£510 (F)

(h)

	£
Budgeted fixed overhead (5,100 units × 2 hrs × £3.70)	37,740
Actual fixed overhead	42,300
Fixed overhead price variance	4,560 (A)

(i)

4,850 combos should have taken (× 2 hrs)	9,700 hrs
but did take	8,000 hrs
Usage variance in hrs	1,700 hrs (F)
× standard rate per hour	× £3.70
Fixed overhead usage variance	£6,290 (F)

(j)

Budgeted activity level (5,100 × 2 hrs)	10,200 hrs
Actual activity level	8,000 hrs
Capacity variance in hrs	2,200 hrs (A)
× standard rate per hour	× £3.70
Fixed overhead capacity variance	£8,140 (A)

Reporting variances

6.5 The report to management may be in the form of the detailed analysis above. In practice you may come across a variety of methods of reporting variances.

6.6 The following, for example, is not uncommon.

CONTROL REPORT

Month   June 19X7
Budgeted output   5,100 units
Actual output   4,850 units

	Actual costs £	Output Units	Standard costs Unit cost £	Total cost £	Total Variance £
Materials	9,800	4,850	2.00	9,700	100 (A)
Labour	16,800	4,850	4.00	19,400	2,600 (F)
Variable overhead	2,600	4,850	0.60	2,910	310 (F)
Fixed overhead	42,300	4,850	7.40	35,890	6,410 (A)
	71,500			67,900	3,600 (A)

6.7 This report effectively compares actual costs with 'flexed' budget figures. This means that the budgeted figures have been recalculated to show what would have been expected if the actual production volume had been known in advance.

6.8 If you compare the total variances shown in the control report with the sum of the individual variances for each type of cost in Paragraph 6.4 you will see that this is a briefer form of the full variance calculations. As an appendix to such a report management could therefore be provided with a breakdown of any large variances, for example the labour variance and the fixed overhead variance.

6.9 Alternatively the variances may form part of an operating statement.

ALTOGETHER LTD - OPERATING STATEMENT JUNE 19X7

	(F) £	(A) £	£
Budgeted profit before sales and administration costs			30,600
Sales variances: price		1,400 (A)	
volume		1,500 (A)	
			2,900 (A)
Actual sales minus the standard cost of sales			27,700
Cost variances			
Materials price		600	
Materials usage	500		
Labour rate	200		
Labour efficiency	3,400		
Labour idle time		1,000	
Variable overhead expenditure		200	
Variable overhead efficiency	510		
Fixed overhead expenditure		4,560	
Fixed overhead volume efficiency	6,290		
Fixed overhead volume capacity		8,140	
	10,900	14,500	3,600 (A)
Actual profit before sales and administration costs			24,100
Sales and administration costs			18,000
Actual profit, June 19X7			6,100

	£	£
Sales		95,600
Materials	9,800	
Labour	16,800	
Variable overhead	2,600	
Fixed overhead	42,300	
Sales and administration	18,000	
		89,500
Profit		6,100

You are not expected to cover sales variances at this level.

7   INVESTIGATING VARIANCES

7.1   Whatever the form reports take and however often they are prepared (monthly, quarterly etc) the reporting system will only be useful if action is taken as a result. It is no use sending reports to management or cost accountants which will never be read.

7.2   Management should review the reports, noting any unusual variances by size or nature that need further investigation. You should remember what is significant will vary according to the variance concerned. It may be, for example, that management investigates all idle time variances. The acceptable variance of material costs, if the market is volatile, may well be greater than the acceptable variance for material usage.

Responsibility for variances

7.3   A key element in investigation will be to speak to the person responsible for the variance, often departmental heads. This does not mean that they will be blamed for the variances; the variances may be due to external factors (for example a material price increase) beyond their control.

7.4   As a general rule, price or expenditure variances will be the responsibility of whoever makes the decision to purchase the resources. For purchases of material for example, responsibility is likely to lie with the purchasing department. The finance director may be responsible for major repairs expenditure. Usage or efficiency variances are likely to be the responsibility of the production department.

7.5   Investigation may demonstrate ,however, that someone, other than the person normally responsible, has taken the decision that has led to the variance. We mentioned earlier in this chapter the example of a production manager who was asked to explain why he had used 1,000 more units than he should have done. The explanation was that the purchasing department had purchased lower quality material, a lot of which had to be thrown away. In these circumstances it is the purchasing department who have caused the adverse usage variance; the required action may be that the purchasing department have to ensure materials of the right quality are purchased in future.

7.6   Similarly the price variance would normally be the responsibility of the purchasing department. However, if bad stock control meant that higher cost materials had to be purchased at short notice, the price variance would be the responsibility of the stores department.

7.7   Once the reasons have been established action will need to be taken. For example, inefficiencies caused by use of low quality material may mean higher quality material should be purchased in the future. Alternatively, if the variance is due to external circumstances (such as unexpected material price rise) future standards may have to be adjusted to take account of this.

8   COST ACCOUNTING ENTRIES FOR VARIANCES
Centrally assessed 6/97

8.1   In a double entry bookkeeping system, all cost variances are recorded in the account where they arise, with the appropriate double entry taken to a variance account. Let us look at material variances as an example.

(a)   Materials price variances are apparent when materials are purchased, and they are therefore recorded in the stores account. If a price variance is adverse, we should credit stores account and debit a variance account with the amount of the variance.

(b)   Materials usage variances do not occur until output is actually produced in the factory, and they are therefore recorded in the work in progress account. If a usage variance is favourable, we should debit the work in progress account and credit a variance account with the amount of the variance (in £).

8.2   Materials are transferred from the stores account to the WIP account at what the actual quantity purchased *should* have cost. If the actual amount paid for the materials (which is a debit on the stores account) is different from this value, there will be a balance remaining on the stores account. This is the materials *price* variance and it is transferred either to a separate account set up specially to collect all variances or to an account specially for materials price variances.

8.3   The materials *usage* variance is included in the WIP account and is determined by valuing the difference between the amount of material actually used and the amount that should have been used at standard cost. Favourable variances are debits and adverse variances credits in the WIP account. This means that the corresponding entries in the variance account (either an account for all variances or one for materials usage variances alone) appear as follows.

VARIANCE ACCOUNT

	£		£
Adverse variances	X	Favourable variances	X
		Balance (to P & L account)	X
	$\overline{\underline{\text{X}}}$		$\overline{\underline{\text{X}}}$

8.4   The same principles apply to other variances. In the previous example of Altogether Ltd, for example, the favourable labour rate variance will be a debit in the direct wages control account and a credit in a variances account. The favourable labour efficiency variance will be a debit in the WIP account and a credit in a variances account.

8.5   The balance of variances in the variance account (whether total variance account or individual variance accounts) at the end of a period is written off to the profit and loss account.

8.6   We will now show what the variance account would look like for Altogether Ltd, whose variances we calculated in Section 6.

VARIANCE ACCOUNT

	£		£
Stores a/c (materials price)	600	WIP a/c (materials usage)	500
WIP a/c (idle time)	1,000	Direct wages a/c (labour rate)	200
Fixed overhead a/c (price)	4,560	WIP a/c (labour efficiency)	3,400
Fixed overhead a/c (capacity)	8,140	WIP a/c (variable o'hd efficiency)	510
Variable o'hd a/c (expenditure)	200	WIP a/c (fixed overhead usage)	6,290
		Profit and loss a/c (balance)	3,600
	$\underline{14,500}$		$\underline{14,500}$

8.7 You may be asked to post the variable overhead or fixed overhead total variances, and you may not be given details of the variances that make up the total variance. If so, you should post the total variance to the variable or fixed overhead control account, the other side of the entry being of course to the variances account.

Deduction of variances

8.8 You may be asked to deduce variances from information you are given.

Example: Deduction of variances

8.9 The cost accountant of General Herbage Ltd has a problem. He knows that the only information left to post in the T accounts below is the materials usage and price variances and the labour rate and efficiency variances. Unfortunately the only variance he has been able to calculate is a £20,000 adverse labour efficiency variance. See if you can deduce the remaining variances and post them correctly to the T accounts.

RAW MATERIALS STORES ACCOUNT

	£000		£000
Balance b/f	70	Work in progress	90
Creditors	120	Balance c/f	90

WAGES AND SALARIES ACCOUNT

	£000		£000
Bank	130	Work in progress	200
Creditor for national insurance and PAYE	40		

WORK IN PROGRESS ACCOUNT

	£000		£000
Raw materials	90	Finished goods	285
Wages and salaries	200		

VARIANCES ACCOUNT

£000	£000

Solution: Deduction of variances

8.10 The balancing entry for the raw materials account must be an adverse *materials price* variance of £10,000.

RAW MATERIALS STORES ACCOUNT

	£000		£000
Balance b/f	70	Work in progress	90
Creditors	120	Variances account – materials price variance	10
		Balance c/f	90
	190		190

8.11 The balancing entry for the wages and salaries account must be a favourable labour rate variance of £30,000.

WAGES AND SALARIES ACCOUNT

	£000		£000
Bank	130	Work in progress	200
Creditor for national insurance and PAYE	40		
Variances account – labour rate variance	30		
	200		200

8.12 The work in progress account lacks the materials usage and labour efficiency variances, but we can post the labour efficiency variance.

WORK IN PROGRESS ACCOUNT

	£000		£000
Raw materials	90	Variances account	20
Wages and salaries	200	- labour efficiency variance	
		Finished goods	285

8.13 This therefore means that the balancing figure on the work in progress account must be a favourable materials usage variance of £15,000.

WORK IN PROGRESS ACCOUNT

	£000		£000
Raw materials	90	Variances account	20
Wages and salaries	200	- labour efficiency variance	
Variances account	15	Finished goods	285
- materials usage variance			
	305		305

8.14 We can therefore complete the variances account.

VARIANCES ACCOUNT

	£000		£000
Labour efficiency variance	20	Materials usage variance	15
Materials price variance	10	Labour rate variance	30
Profit and loss account	15		
	45		45

Key points in this chapter

- A total materials variance can be divided into a price variance and a usage variance.

- A total labour variance can be divided into a rate variance and an efficiency variance.

- Adverse variances mean less profit than we hoped, favourable variance more profit.

- Fixed overhead variances are calculated to explain the reasons for any under- or over-absorbed overhead. The total variance can be split into price, usage and capacity variances.

- The reasons for cost variances are diverse: full information should be obtained from those directly involved before any reprimand is dealt out for adverse variances or praise is given for favourable ones.

- The point of calculating variances is to report them to management, who can then take action. There are various forms reports can take.

- In a double entry bookkeeping system, all cost variances are recorded in the account where they arise, with the appropriate double entry taken to a variance account.

For practice on the points covered in this chapter you should now attempt the Exercises in Session 9 of the Cost Information Workbook

Index

ORDER FORM

Any books from our AAT range can be ordered by telephoning 0181-740 2211. Alternatively, send this page to our Freepost address or fax it to us on 0181-740 1184.

To: BPP Publishing Ltd, FREEPOST, London W12 8BR   **Tel: 0181-740 2211**
Fax: 0181-740 1184

Forenames (Mr / Ms): _____

Surname: _____

Address: _____

_____

Post code: _____

Please send me the following books (all editions are 8/97 unless otherwise stated):

		Price Interactive Text £	Kit £	Quantity Interactive Text	Kit	Total £
Foundation						
Unit 1	Cash Transactions	9.95		....		....
Unit 2	Credit Transactions	9.95		....		....
Unit 1 & 2	Cash & Credit Transactions Devolved Ass'mt		9.95		....	....
Unit 1 & 2	Cash & Credit Transactions Central Ass'mt		9.95		....	....
Unit 3	Payroll Transactions (9/97)	9.95		....		....
Unit 3	Payroll Transactions Devolved Ass'mt (9/97)		9.95		....	....
Unit 20	Data Processing (DOS) (7/95)	9.95*		....		....
Unit 20	Data Processing (Windows)	9.95		....		....
Units 24-28	Business Knowledge	9.95		....		....

		Tutorial Text	Workbook	Tutorial Text	Workbook	
Intermediate						
Units 4&5	Financial Accounting	10.95	10.95	....	....	....
Unit 6	Cost Information	10.95	10.95	....	....	....
Units 7&8	Reports and Returns	10.95	10.95	....	....	....
Units 21&22	Information Technology	10.95*		....		
Technician						
Unit 9	Cash Management & Credit Control	10.95	8.95	....	....	....
Unit 10	Managing Accounting Systems	10.95	6.95	....	....	....
Units 11,12&13	Management Accounting	16.95	10.95	....	....	....
Unit 14	Financial Statements	10.95	8.95	....	....	....
Unit 18	Auditing	10.95	6.95	....	....	....
Unit 19	Taxation (FA 97) (10/97)	10.95	8.95	....	....	....
Unit 23	Information Management Systems	10.95	6.95	....	....	....
Units 10,18&23	Project Guidance		6.95		....	....
Unit 25	Health and Safety at Work	3.95**		....		....

* Combined Text

**Price includes postage; this booklet is an extract from Units
24-28 Business Knowledge (Interactive Text)

Postage & packaging:

UK: £2.00 for first plus £2.00 for each extra book.   ....

Europe (inc ROI): £4.00 for first plus £2.00 for each extra book.   ....

Rest of the World: £6.00 for first plus £4.00 for each extra book.   ....

Total _____

I enclose a cheque for £ _____ or charge to Access/Visa/Switch

Card number | | | | | | | | | | | | | | | | |

Start date (Switch only) _____ Expiry date _____ Issue no. (Switch only) _____

Signature _____

REVIEW FORM & FREE PRIZE DRAW

All original review forms from the entire BPP range, completed with genuine comments, will be entered into one of two draws on 31 January 1998 and 31 July 1998. The names on the first four forms picked out on each occasion will be sent a cheque for £50.

Name: _____   Address: _____

_____

_____

How have you used this Tutorial Text?
(Tick one box only)

☐ Home study (book only)

☐ On a course: college _____

☐ With 'correspondence' package

☐ Other _____

Why did you decide to purchase this Tutorial Text? *(Tick one box only)*

☐ Have used complementary Workbook

☐ Have used BPP Texts in the past

☐ Recommendation by friend/colleague

☐ Recommendation by a lecturer at college

☐ Saw advertising

☐ Other _____

During the past six months do you recall seeing/receiving any of the following?
(Tick as many boxes as are relevant)

☐ Our advertisement in *Accounting Technician* Magazine

☐ Our advertisement in *PASS*

☐ Our brochure with a letter through the post

Which (if any) aspects of our advertising do you find useful?
(Tick as many boxes as are relevant)

☐ Prices and publication dates of new editions

☐ Information on Tutorial Text content

☐ Facility to order books off-the-page

☐ None of the above

Have you used the companion Workbook for this subject?   ☐ Yes   ☐ No

Your ratings, comments and suggestions would be appreciated on the following areas

	Very useful	Useful	Not useful
Introductory section (How to use this Tutorial Text, etc)	☐	☐	☐
Coverage of elements of competence	☐	☐	☐
Examples	☐	☐	☐
Index	☐	☐	☐
Structure and presentation	☐	☐	☐

	Excellent	Good	Adequate	Poor
Overall opinion of this Tutorial Text	☐	☐	☐	☐

Do you intend to continue using BPP Tutorial Texts/Workbooks?   ☐ Yes   ☐ No

Please note any further comments and suggestions/errors on the reverse of this page

Please return to: Neil Biddlecombe, BPP Publishing Ltd, FREEPOST, London, W12 8BR

REVIEW FORM & FREE PRIZE DRAW (continued)
Please note any further comments and suggestions/errors below